Guide to Japan

Wining and Dining
the Japanese Way

Boye De Mente is an acknowledged
authority on the Orient and the author
of more than 30 books. *Diner's Guide to
Japan* is his third in the Japan Quick-
Guide series. He first came to Japan
in 1949 with the U.S. Army Security
Agency and has been involved with
Japan as a journalist, editor, lecturer,
and writer ever since.

Other Books by Boye De Mente

Diner's
Guide to Japan

Wining and Dining
the Japanese Way

by

Boye Lafayette De Mente

YENBOOKS are published and distributed
by the Charles E. Tuttle Company, Inc.
of Rutland, Vermont & Tokyo, Japan
with editorial offices at
2-6 Suido 1-chome, Bunkyo-ku, Tokyo 112

LCC Card No. 89-51720
ISBN 0-8048-1641-7

First printing, 1990

Printed in Japan

Contents

Contents

Contents

Contents

Contents

Preface

Until recently the international image of Japanese food tended to be an unflattering stereotype based on the idea that rice and raw fish were the mainstays of the Japanese diet. Many people felt that these dishes were indicative of the rest of the country's traditional cuisine. While Japanese cuisine is still not generally well-known abroad, today more people are aware that Japanese food includes a variety of cooking styles, and many know that traditional Japanese food is low in cholesterol, low in fat and calories, and high in fiber.

Like all cuisines, Japanese food is a product of the culture that produced it. Feudal Japan was divided into regions by distance, high mountains, the ocean, and rigid political constraints. Travel between regions was strictly limited, forcing inhabitants to become virtually self-sufficient. This division of the country led to the development of distinctive, regional differences in diet and cooking styles, many of which continue to exist today.

Climate was another factor in the development of Japanese cuisine. In fact, Japan's traditional culture is often described as a seasonal culture because so much of it revolves around the changing seasons. The overall Japanese diet remains closely attuned to the seasons, and even today one must follow age-old customs to be accepted as an intelligent diner.

Despite the development of over a hundred regional cuisines during Japan's long feudal age, there were always a number of common characteristics that identified the various cuisines as Japanese. If you ask a Japanese what makes a food Japanese, he or she will invariably answer *shōyu* (show-yuu), the dark liquid condiment made from fermented soybeans and salt and known as soy sauce in English. A secondary response would probably be that Japanese food is "natural."

I have always thought of *shōyu* as the "taste of Japan" and long ago learned to appreciate its contribution to the many Japanese dishes that tend to be bland in their natural state. At the same time, I found that many of the dishes that Japanese would not think of eating without *shōyu* are very good without it, and often more suitable to Western taste buds.

There is a huge diversity to Japanese food. From Hokkaido's snowy mountains to Okinawa's sandy beaches, people using dozens of cooking styles prepare thousands of different dishes. The country also has an extraordinarily large number of restaurants. Various reasons are given for the number and variety of restaurants, but one important reason is that throughout Japan's history the small, family-run shop has been the primary business structure. Hundreds of thousands of tiny food stalls and restaurants have long been a vital part of this tradition. One of the most conspicuous facets of life in Japan today is the presence of so many public eating places offering different kinds of food. The newcomer faces a formidable challenge in trying to identify the various types of restaurants and making rational dining choices once inside.

This book attempts to meet that challenge by identifying different categories of restaurants, describing their character and appearance, covering the specific dishes they carry, and providing enough Japanese to allow anyone to function effectively in the various types of restaurants. From your very first day in Japan you can order your favorite foods and drinks in Japanese.

Cheers! Or, as the Japanese say, *"Kanpai!"*

Note on Pronunciation

The six key sounds of Japanese are represented by the English letters *a, i, u, e, o,* and *n*. The five vowels in Japanese are pronounced as follows:

a	as in f*a*ther
i	as in Bal*i*
u	as in tr*u*e
e	as in pr*e*ss
o	as in c*o*lt

These vowels and the *n* sound are "syllables" in themselves, and the vowels also combine with consonants to produce all the other Japanese syllables. For example, the five vowel sounds plus the consonant *k* combine to produce *ka, ki, ku, ke,* and *ko,* pronounced "kah, kee, kuu, kay," and "koh."

Long vowels are pronounced twice as long as regular vowels and are marked *ā, ī, ū, ē,* and *ō*. Most syllables in Japanese are distinctly pronounced. At times, however, the *i* and *u* vowel sounds are weak and not clearly pronounced. Thus, the word *desu* becomes "dess" and *yoroshiku* becomes "yo-rosh-ku."

In this book, Japanese words are first written in the modified Hepburn romanization system, with long vowels indicated by a macron. This is followed by the phonetic spelling used in the other Quick-Guides, a system readily understandable even by those encountering Japanese for the first time.

1

Dining Etiquette

One of the things for which Japan is noted is its highly refined, sophisticated etiquette. Until recently this etiquette covered virtually every aspect of life—how one slept, sat, ate, walked, worked—and was strictly followed. While etiquette today is far less strict than it was just a few decades ago, enough of it remains to set the Japanese apart from other people, and to present a challenge to visitors trying to operate successfully in Japan.

When dining Japanese style there are a number of etiquette pointers that visitors need to know. These are not absolutely crucial matters that always have to be adhered to, but knowing just a few points can help you avoid making negative impressions and make you feel more comfortable.

1. At formal or semiformal gatherings, don't begin eating until the host or someone else in charge gives the signal.

2. Don't attempt to use your chopsticks as a knife and fork. If you cannot use chopsticks, it is all right to ask for a *naifu* (nie-fuu) and *fōku* (foe-kuu).

3. It is all right to pick up your rice bowl and hold it under your chin when you are eating. It is also proper to use your rice bowl as a tray or safety net when eating other foods with chopsticks. You can place other food on top of the rice and raise the bowl up, or hold the bowl like a tray as you bring each bite to your mouth. Of course, you cannot eat soup with chopsticks, so it is necessary to drink from soup bowls. But some soups require stirring with chopsticks because the ingredients settle to the bottom.

4. Chopsticks used in Chinese restaurants are larger and heavier than Japanese chopsticks, and some people find them much more difficult to use. If you are dining at a Chinese restaurant and are not adept at using the larger chopsticks, it is permissible to ask for the lightweight Japanese chopsticks called *waribashi* (wah-ree-bah-she). These wooden chopsticks, which you split apart before using, are disposable.

5. It is good manners to stop eating and lay your

chopsticks down while you are being served something. When receiving a bowl of rice or other dish from someone, it is polite to use both hands.

6. It is customary to pour drinks for others as a gesture of goodwill, respect, etc., particularly if you are the host. In a formal setting the host may get up from his seat to pour drinks for other guests around the room.

7. When someone offers you more beer or saké, it is polite to pick up the glass or cup and hold it in both hands, one hand on the bottom and the other steadying the side.

8. The Japanese are extraordinarily hospitable, even aggressive, about paying bills in bars and restaurants, even when it is not their turn. Many visitors, out of embarrassment—or maybe relief—do not insist on paying the bill, allowing the Japanese members to pay. If it is your turn to pay and you want to avoid an unpleasant struggle for the bill, get up from the table early, as if you are going to the restroom, pay the bill, then return to the party.

9. In small Japanese-style or neighborhood Chinese-style restaurants, water or napkins are not automatically set out on the table. At all restaurants, water will be served if it is asked

for, and some restaurants will provide napkins on request.

10. If you have a problem sitting on the floor for a prolonged time, it is acceptable to ask for a *za-isu* (zah-ee-sue), which is basically a chair without legs that provides support for one's back.

2

Ingredients and Cooking Styles

Many visitors to Japan are reluctant to try unfamiliar food because they fear it may be made of something they consider inedible or weird. Food does have a strong psychological as well as physiological impact on everyone, so it is natural to be wary of unusual foods. One of the purposes of this book is to remove some of the mystery from Japanese cuisine.

Although sushi is eaten raw, most Japanese foods are cooked or pickled, and most ingredients are common to many other cuisines. The main ingredients in Japanese dishes are rice, buckwheat and wheat noodles, seafood and sea plants, a variety of vegetables and roots, eggs, beef, pork, and chicken. These are flavored with vinegar, salt, and the ubiquitous soy sauce, *shōyu* (show-yuu). Fruits, nuts, and various plant and tree leaves are also part of the Japanese diet. Like virtually everything else in Japan, Japanese food has been meticulously classified and categorized into styles of cooking, kinds of food, and types of restaurants. Following is a list of the main preparation styles:

broiled dishes *yaki-mono* (yah-kee-moe-no)
deep-fried dishes *age-mono* (ah-gay-moe-no)
dishes served in sauce *ae-mono* (aye-moe-no)
one-pot stews *nabe-mono* (nah-bay-moe-no)
raw seafood *sashimi* (sah-she-me)
soups *sui-mono* (sue-e-moe-no)
steamed dishes *mushi-mono* (muu-she-moe-no)
stewed dishes *ni-mono* (nee-moe-no)

3

Types of Food in Japan

Because of the extraordinary variety of restaurants and drinking places, their unusual outward appearance, and the language barrier, identifying a particular type of shop can be a challenge. Signs, besides being written in Japanese, may be small, inconspicuous, or even nonexistent. Learning to recognize the familiar fronts of different types of restaurants, plus learning to recognize a few common signs written in Japanese, can help you identify different types of shops. Following is a list of the main types of restaurants and foods, along with their names written in Japanese:

bar *bā* (bah) バー

beef and vegetables cooked in thin broth *shabu-shabu* (shah-buu-shah-buu) しゃぶしゃぶ

box lunch *o-bentō* (oh-ben-toe) お弁当

buckwheat noodles *soba* (so-bah) そば

charcoal-grilled food *robata-yaki* (roe-bah-tah-yah-kee) 炉端焼

Chinese food *chūgoku ryōri* (chuu-go-kuu rio-ree) 中国料理

Chinese noodles *rāmen* (rah-men) ラーメン

Chinese-style food *chūka ryōri* (chuu-kah rio-ree) 中華料理

coffee shop *kōhī-ten* (koe-he-ten) コーヒー店; *kōhī-shoppu* (koe-he-shope-puu) コーヒー・ショップ

formal Japanese restaurant *kaiseki ryōri-ya* (kie-say-kee rio-ree-yah) 会席料理屋

fried dumplings *gyōza* (g'yoe-zah) ギョーザ

Japanese a la carte restaurant *koryōri-ya* (koe-rio-ree-yah) 小料理屋

Japanese cooking *nihon ryōri* (nee-hoan rio-ree) 日本料理

Japanese food *washoku* (wah-show-kuu) 和食

Japanese stew *oden* (oh-den) おでん

Japanese-style grilled meat *teppan-yaki* (tep-pahn-yah-kee) 鉄板焼

Korean barbecue *yaki-niku* (yah-kee-nee-kuu) 焼肉

one-pot stew *nabe-mono* (nah-bay-moe-no) 鍋物

pork cutlet, breaded and deep-fried *ton-katsu* (tone-kot-sue) とんカツ

pub *pabu* (pah-buu) パブ

skewered, deep-fried food *kushi-age* (kuu-she-ah-gay) 串上げ

skewered, grilled chicken chunks *yaki-tori* (yah-ke-toe-ree) 焼鳥

skewered, grilled meat, vegetable, etc. *kushi-yaki* (kuu-she-yah-kee) 串焼

small bar serving food *sunakku* (sue-nahk-kuu) スナック

sukiyaki *suki-yaki* (sue-kee-yah-kee) すき焼

sushi *sushi* (suu-she) 寿司

tea and coffee shop *kissa-ten* (keece-sah-ten) 喫茶店

tempura *tenpura* (ten-puu-rah) 天婦羅

traditional tea house *kanmi-kissa* (kahn-me-kee-sah) 甘味喫茶

vegetarian restaurant *saishoku resutoran* (sie-show-kuu res-toe-rahn) 菜食レストラン ; *shōjin ryōri-ya* (show-jeen rio-ree-yah) 精進料理屋

Western food *yōshoku* (yoe-show-kuu) 洋食

Western-style food *seiyō ryōri* (say-yoe rio-ree) 西洋料理

wheat noodles *udon* (uu-doan) うどん

Following are signs and labels you are apt to encounter in and around restaurants in Japan:

brown, sweet sauce (for pork cutlet) *sōsu* (so-sue) ソース

closed *kyūgyō-chū* (que-g'yoe-chuu) 休業中

closed right now *junbi-chū* (june-bee-chuu) 準備中

emergency exit *hijōguchi* (he-joe-guu-chee) 非常口

entrance *iriguchi* (ee-ree-guu-chee) 入口

exit *deguchi* (day-guu-chee) 出口

men *otoko* (oh-toe-koe) 男

open *eigyō-chū* (egg-yoe-chuu) 営業中

restroom *o-tearai* (oh-tay-ah-rye) お手洗い

soy sauce *shōyu* (show-yuu) しょう油

today's special *honjitsu no o-susume* (hoan-jeet-sue no oh-sue-sue-may) 本日のおすすめ

women *onna* (own-nah) 女

4

The Noren Sign

Several hundred years ago Japanese shopkeepers and restaurateurs developed the practice of hanging short, indigo-colored curtains across the fronts of their shops as banners bearing the name of the shop or the kind of food served. These curtains, which provided some privacy and helped keep dust and flies out, were called *noren* (no-ren). As the generations passed, the *noren* of famous shops came to be recognized as their logos, as the "face" they presented to the public. Today many restaurants continue to use *noren*. Shopkeepers hang out their curtain to show they are open; they remove the curtain to indicate they are closed.

5

Basic Terms

Two expressions have become ritualized over the centuries and remain important elements in Japanese dining etiquette. These are *itadakimasu* (ee-tah-dah-kee-mahss) and *go-chisō-sama deshita* (go-chee-so-sah-mah desh-tah).

Itadakimasu is said before you begin to eat. By itself the word means receive or accept, and in earlier days no doubt was an expression of gratitude, meaning something like "I accept the food you are offering me." Its deeper, more solemn implications have lessened considerably, often to the point that today it means little more than "I'm going to dig in!" Use of *itadakimasu*, however, is practically mandatory when someone is treating you, even for something as simple as a beer or sandwich.

Go-chisō-sama deshita is said after you finish eating, to your host after he or she pays the bill, and generally to the restaurant staff as you leave a shop. By itself *go-chisō* means entertainment, meal, or some other enjoyable experience. *Sama* is a very polite way of saying Mr., Mrs., or Miss. *Deshita* is the past tense of the verb be. Together *go-chisō-sama deshita* means something like "Thank you very much for the meal or entertainment." Saying *go-chisō-sama* to the restaurant staff as you leave is simply a polite gesture.

Following are other basic terms you may find useful when dining out in Japan:

food *tabe-mono* (tah-bay-moe-no)

drink; beverage *nomi-mono* (no-me-moe-no)

Japanese food *nihon ryōri* (nee-hoan rio-ree); *washoku* (wah-show-kuu)

Western-style food *yōshoku* (yoe-show-kuu)

breakfast *asa gohan* (ah-sah go-hahn)

lunch *hiru gohan* (hee-rue go-hahn)

dinner *yūshoku* (yuu-show-kuu)

reservation *yoyaku* (yoe-yah-kuu)

restaurant *shokudō* (show-kuu-doe)

Japanese-style room where you sit on tatami mats *zashiki* (zah-she-kee)

legless chair used on tatami floors *za-isu* (zah-ee-sue)

table *tēburu* (tay-buu-rue)

chair *isu* (ee-sue)

chopsticks *o-hashi* (oh-hah-she)

disposable, wooden chopsticks that pull apart *waribashi* (wah-ree-bah-she)

knife *naifu* (nie-fuu)

fork *fōku* (foe-kuu)

napkin *napukin* (nah-puu-keen)

dampened hand towel *o-shibori* (oh-she-boe-ree)

set meal *teishoku* (tay-show-kuu)

set breakfast, usually very light, like coffee, toast, an egg, etc. *mōningu-sābisu* (moe-neen-guu-sah-bee-sue) course *kōsu* (koe-sue)

a la carte *ippin ryōri* (eep-peen rio-ree)

snack item (e.g., peanuts) served automatically in bars and clubs *o-tōshi* (o-toh-she)

menu *menyū* (men-yuu)

order *chūmon* (chuu-moan)

meal ticket purchased in advance that indicates the dish you want *shokken* (shoak-ken) (Note: Hand the ticket to the waiter or waitress.)

more *motto* (moat-toe)

a little bit *sukoshi* (sue-koe-she)

enough *mō takusan* (moe tock-sahn)

full *ippai* (eep-pie)

water *mizu* (mee-zoo)

vegetable *yasai* (yah-sie)

soy sauce *shōyu* (show-yuu)

vinegar *su* (sue)

pepper *koshō* (koe-show)

salt *shio* (she-oh)

spicy hot *karai* (kah-rye)

hot (to the touch) *atsui* (aht-sue-e)

cool or cold (to the touch) *tsumetai* (t'sue-may-tie)

counter *kauntā* (koun-tah)

shopping arcade *ākēdo* (ah-kay-doe)

street lined with shops and restaurants *shotengai* (show-ten-guy)

check *o-kanjō* (oh-kahn-joe)

together (all on one check) *issho* (ees-show)

separate (checks) *betsu-betsu* (bet-sue-bet-sue)

check, please *o-kanjō kudasai* (oh-kahn-joe kuu-dah-sie)
service charge *sābisu-ryō* (sah-bee-suu-rio)
delivery service *demae* (day-my)
takeout food *omochi-kaeri* (oh-moe-chee-kie-ree)

6

Expressions You Will Hear

The expressions you hear in a Japanese restaurant are fairly standard. They include the following:

Irasshaimase! (Ee-rah-shy-mah-say!) Welcome! ˙

Nan mei sama desu ka? (Nahn may-e sah-mah dess kah?) How many of you are there?

O-hitori desu ka? (Oh-ssh-toe-ree dess kah?) Are you by yourself? (Note: The *h* in *hitori* is often pronounced *sh.*)

O-futari desu ka? (Oh-fuu-tah-ree dess kah?) Are there two of you?

Sannin desu ka? (Sahn-neen dess kah?) Are there three of you?

Kochira e, dōzo. (Koe-chee-rah eh, doe-zoe.) This way, please.

O-kimari ni narimashita ka? (Oh-kee-mah-ree nee nah-ree-mahssh-tah kah?) Have you decided (what to order)?

Nani ni nasaimasu ka? (Nahn nee nah-sie-mahss kah?)
What will you have?

O-nomi-mono wa nani ni itashimashō? (Oh-no-me-moe-no
wah nahn nee ee-tah-she-mah-show?) What would
you like to drink?

O-sage shite yoroshii deshō ka? (Oh-sah-gay ssh-tay yoe-
roe-shee day-show kah?) Is it all right to clear (these
dishes) away?

Dō-mo arigatō gozaimasu. (Doe-moe ah-ree-gah-toe go-
zie-mahss.) Thank you very much.

7

Expressions You Will Use

Following are some basic
expressions you are likely to use in restaurants:

Hitori desu. (Ssh-toe-ree dess.) I'm by myself.

Futari desu. (Fuu-tah-ree dess.) There are two of us.

Sannin desu. (Sahn-neen dess.) There are three of us.

Tabako no kinshi basho ga arimasu ka? (Tah-bah-koe no
keen-she bah-show gah ah-ree-mahss kah?) Do you
have a no-smoking area?

Sumimasen! (Sue-me-mah-sen!) Excuse me! (Note: This
word is used to attract the attention of a waiter or
waitress.)

Menyū o itadakemasu ka? (Men-yuu oh e-tah-dah-kay-
mahss kah?) May I have a menu, please?

Mōningu-sābisu, kudasai. (Moe-neen-guu-sah-be-sue, kuu-dah-sie.) Please bring me the morning set.

The word *kudasai* can be very useful when wining and dining in Japan. By adding *kudasai* to whatever you want to eat or drink, you are saying "Please bring me _____."

Kōhī, kudasai. (Koe-he, kuu-dah-sie.) Coffee, please.

Mizu, kudasai. (Mee-zuu, kuu-dah-sie.) Water, please.

O-kanjō, kudasai. (Oh-kahn-joe, kuu-dah-sie.) Check, please.

Another useful word is *arimasu* (ah-ree-mahss), meaning have, and its interrogative form, *arimasu ka,* meaning "Do you have _____?"

Aisu-kurīmu arimasu ka? (Aye-sue-kuu-ree-muu ah-ree-mahss kah?) Do you have ice cream?

Pan arimasu ka? (Pahn ah-ree-mahss kah?) Do you have bread?

A third useful term is *nan-no* (nahn-no), which means what kind.

Nan-no aisu-kurīmu arimasu ka? (Nahn-no aye-sue-kuu-ree-muu ah-ree-mahss kah?) What kind of ice cream do you have?

Nan-no bīru arimasu ka? (Nahn-no bee-rue ah-ree-mahss kah?) What kind of beer do you have?

Nan-no teishoku arimasu ka? (Nahn-no tay-show-kuu ah-ree-mahss kah?) What kind of set meals do you have?

8

Counting in Japanese

The Japanese counting system is a bit complicated because different words are used for different shaped objects. However, with the following list of numbers you should be able to order what you want.

1 *hitotsu* (he-toe-t'sue)
2 *futatsu* (fuu-tah-t'sue)
3 *mittsu* (meet-sue)
4 *yottsu* (yoat-sue)
5 *itsutsu* (ee-t'sue-t'sue)
6 *muttsu* (moot-sue)
7 *nanatsu* (nah-naht-sue)
8 *yattsu* (yaht-sue)
9 *kokonotsu* (koe-koe-no-t'sue)
10 *tō* (toe)

Unlike in English, in Japanese, the number follows the thing you want.

Hanbāgā o yotsu kudasai. (Hahm-bah-gah oh yoat-sue kuu-dah-sie.) Four hamburgers, please.

Kōhī o mittsu kudasai. (Koe-he oh meet-sue kuu-dah-sie.) Three cups of coffee, please.

O-bentō o futatsu kudasai. (Oh-ben-toe oh fuu-tah-t'sue kuu-dah-sie.) Two box lunches, please.

9

Set Meals

Most Japanese-style restaurants and some Western-style restaurants have a selection of set meals for breakfast, lunch, and dinner. The generic term for such meals is *teishoku* (tay-show-kuu), but there are several other terms in use as well.

Mōningu-setto (moe-neen-guu-set-toe), literally "morning set," served in Western-style coffee shops and some bakeries, is a light breakfast of coffee and toast, a hard-boiled egg, a small salad, etc. In some Japanese-style restaurants a *mōningu-setto* is a bowl of rice, *miso* (bean paste) soup, grilled fish, and Japanese pickles. The set breakfast is also called *mōningu-sābisu* (moe-neen-guu-sah-bee-sue), literally "morning service." The Japanese word *sābisu* means something that is given free or at a discount.

A lunch special, *ranchi-supesharu* (rahn-chee-sue-pay-shah-rue), is a full meal in both Japanese and Western-style restaurants, although in some places, this may consist of a single large dish, such as rice topped with meat and vegetables. The term *ranchi-sābisu* (rahn-chee-sah-bee-sue), "lunch service," is also commonly used.

Kyō no aji (k'yoe no ah-jee), literally the "taste of today," is a full-course meal offered at lunch and dinner by some Japanese-style restaurants. *Kyō no susume* (k'yoe no sue-sue-may) means today's recommendation.

There are also specials like *kēki-setto* (kay-kee-set-toe), cake and coffee at a price that is twenty to thirty percent below what the two would cost if ordered separately.

10

Soft Drinks

Japan has a wide variety of nonalcoholic drinks, some familiar and others unique. Many are available in vending machines. Among the most common are the following:

apple drink *ringo jūsu* (reen-go juu-suu)

black or brown tea, usually served with a lemon slice or milk *kōcha* (koe-chah)

Calpis (kah-rue-pee-sue) a sweet milky drink

Coca-Cola *Kokakōra* (koe-kah-koe-rah)

coffee *kōhī* (koe-hee) Plain coffee. Japan has many coffee shops that offer a variety of coffee blends. There are no free refills in Japanese coffee shops.

cola float *kōra furōto* (koe-rah fuu-roe-toe) cola with a scoop of vanilla ice cream

cream soda *kurīmu soda* (kuu-ree-muu soe-dah) a green-colored soda with a scoop of vanilla ice cream grape drink *gurēpu jūsu* (guu-ray-puu juu-suu)

Guronsan *Guronsan* (guu-roan-sahn) a vitamin tonic mostly sold at station kiosks

hot chocolate *kokoa* (koe-koe-ah)

iced coffee *aisu kōhī* (aye-sue koe-hee) chilled coffee with ice cubes, usually presweetened

lemon squash *remon sukasshu* (ray-moan suu-kahs-shuu) a sweet soda, usually with a cherry and lemon slice

melon juice *meron jūsu* (may-roan juu-suu) a green, melon-flavored drink

milk *miruku* (me-ruu-kuu) Milk in a Western-style restaurant is usually served cold. In Japanese-style places, it may be served hot in a cup, like coffee, if you do not specify cold milk. Hot milk is *hotto miruku* (hot-toe me-ruu-kuu); cold milk is *tsumetai miruku* (t'sue-may-tie me-ruu-kuu). The original Japanese term for milk is *gyūnyū* (g'yuu-knew).

milk shake *miruku seki* (me-rue-kuu say-kee) a Japanese-style milk shake made with egg, sugar, and milk

orange float *orenji furōto* (oh-ren-jee fuu-roe-toe) a carbonated orange drink with a scoop of ice cream

orange juice *orenji jūsu* (oh-ren-jee juu-suu) Unless specified as "fresh," this is usually a carbonated orange drink. Some hotels have genuine orange juice, *furesshu orenji jūsu* (fuu-ray-shuu oh-ren-jee juu-suu). The term *nama orenji jūsu* (nah-mah oh-ren-jee juu-suu) is also used.

pineapple drink *pain jūsu* (pine juu-suu) usually a carbonated drink unless specified as "fresh"

strawberry juice *ichigo jūsu* (ee-chee-go juu-suu) a drink made from strawberry syrup

tomato juice *tomato jūsu* (toe-mah-toe juu-suu)

11

Ordering Tea

Despite the inroads made by coffee and various kinds of soft drinks, tea remains one of the most popular beverages in Japan. The two most common types of tea are brown or black tea called *kōcha* (koe-chah), served straight or with lemon or milk, and green tea called *o-cha,* which means tea. The two grades of green tea are *sencha* (sen-chah), which is served in better restaurants and is what one would serve guests, and *bancha* (bahn-chah), the cheaper, slightly astringent tea that is made from older leaves and that is served free in many restaurants. Other similar drinks include the following:

genmaicha (gen-my-chah) a drink made from roasted (popped) rice and the leaves used in making cheap green tea

mugicha (muu-ghee-chah) a drink made from roasted barley

hōjicha (hoe-jee-chah) a drink made from roasted *bancha* leaves

konbucha (kone-buu-chah) a salty drink made from powdered sea tangle

matcha (mot-chah) a dark green, powdered tea used

12

Alcoholic Drinks

Many alcoholic drinks popular in Western countries are also found in Japan. Useful vocabulary for ordering beer follows:

beer *bīru* (bee-rue)
draft beer *nama bīru* (nah-mah bee-rue)
dark draft beer *kuro nama bīru* (kuu-roe nah-mah bee-rue)
large bottle *ō-bin* (oh-bean)
medium-sized bottle *chū-bin* (chuu-bean)
small bottle *ko-bin* (koe-bean)
light beer *raito bīru* (rye-toe bee-rue)

Following are useful expressions for ordering other drinks:

bottle (a bottle of liquor reserved in your name) *botoru* (boe-toe-rue)
bourbon *bābon* (bah-bone)
club soda *tansan* (tahn-sahn)
gin *jin* (jeen)
gin tonic *jin-tonikku* (jeen-toe-neek-kuu)
ginger ale *jinjā-ēru* (jeen-jah-ay-rue)
highball *haibōru* (hie-boe-rue)

ice *kōri* (koe-ree); *aisu* (aye-sue)

on-the-rocks *on-za-rokku* (own-zah-roak-kuu)

martini *matīni* (mah-tee-nee)

Perrier mineral water *Perie* (pay-ree-ay)

saké *sake* (sah-kay); *o-sake* (oh-sah-kay); *nihon-shu* (nee-hoan-shuu)

scotch and soda *soda-wari* (soe-dah-wah-ree)

scotch whiskey *sukotchi* (skoe-chee)

shochu (distilled rice or grain liquor) *shōchū* (show-chuu)

tonic water *tonikku-uōtā* (toe-neek-kuu-wah-tah)

vodka *uokka* (wahk-kah)

vodka tonic *uokka-tonikku* (wahk-kah-toe-neek-kuu)

whiskey *uisuki* (we-ski)

whiskey and water *mizu-wari* (mee-zuu-wah-ree)

wine *budō-shu* (buu-doe-shuu); *wain* (wine)

wine, red *aka wain* (ah-kah wine)

wine, white *shiro wain* (she-roe wine)

wine by the glass *gurasu wain* (guu-rah-suu wine)

13

Boxed Food

Japan has a long history of box lunches, *eki-ben*, (ay-kee-ben), originally made for travelers and sold at or near train stations. Over the decades *eki-ben* specialties of some stations became nationally famous, resulting in the appearance of *eki-ben* shops and counters in the food sections of department stores. Several of Tokyo's leading department stores hold annual *eki-ben* fairs featuring thirty or forty of the best-known varieties.

Most *eki-ben* are strictly Japanese style—fish, vegetables, and meat, raw, pickled, or baked, with lots of rice—but some feature chicken, pork, and other familiar ingredients prepared more or less Western style. Small, thin hors d'oeuvre-like sandwiches on trimmed white bread are also common box lunches. In addition to being sold in station retail shops and on station platforms, *eki-ben* are also sold by vendors who go up and down the aisles of trains.

Eating *eki-ben* is a custom in Japan, and is considered part of the fun and adventure of traveling. Many returning travelers bring famous *eki-ben* home with them as souvenirs. Following are some well-known *eki-ben* and the stations that sell them:

chūka bentō (chu-kah ben-toe) Chinese food, including such things as egg roll, fried chicken, sliced pork, etc., with rolls of white rice. Nagasaki Station.

Hakata sanshoku bentō (hah-kah-tah sahn-show-kuu ben-toe) Three separate tiers containing chicken and rice, sushi on rice, and assorted ingredients like shrimp, fish cake, etc., on rice. *Sanshoku* means three colors and the three tiers are each a different color. Hakata Station.

kiku-zake bentō (kee-kuu-zah-kay ben-toe) Famous products of Kanazawa (sea bream wrapped in bamboo leaf, sweet shrimp, cooked walnuts, etc.) and two small bottles of saké, one sweet and one dry. Kanazawa Station.

matsuri-zushi (mot-sue-ree-zuu-she) Pieces of fish (Spanish mackerel, gizzard shad, etc.) from the Inland Sea and mountain vegetables served on rice. Okayama Station.

shamoji kaki meshi (shah-moe-jee kah-kee may-she) Grilled and fried oysters on rice in a container shaped like a *shamoji,* a rice scoop. Hiroshima Station, November through March.

tenzaru soba (ten-zah-ru so-ba) Shrimp, squash, and leaf of the beefsteak plant fixed tempura style, buckwheat noodles, and dipping sauce. Nagano Station.

unagi meshi (uu-nah-ghee may-she) Charcoal-grilled eel, burdock root, and pickles on rice. Toyohashi Station.

yaki-niku bentō (yah-kee-nee-kuu ben-toe) Grilled meat and vegetables on rice. Kyoto Station.

Following are varieties of box lunches sold in places like sports stadiums, convenience stores, etc.:

chicken and egg over rice *oyako-don* (oh-yah-koe-doan)

curry gravy over rice *karē raisu* (kah-ray rye-sue)

deep-fried chicken *kara-age* (kah-rah-ah-gay)

deep-fried ground-meat patty *menchi-katsu* (men-chee-kot-sue)

deep-fried pork cutlet *ton-katsu* (tone-kot-sue)

dried seaweed on a bed of rice *nori bentō* (no-ree ben-toe) fried beef patty, shrimp, and croquette *mikkusu furai* (meek-sue fuu-rye)

fried shrimp *ebi furai* (ay-bee fuu-rye)

grilled eel *unagi* (uu-nah-ghee)

grilled marinated meat with rice *yaki-niku* (yah-kee-nee-kuu)

hamburger patty in gravy *hanbāgu* (hahn-bah-guu)

minute steak *sutēki* (sue-tay-kee)

pork cutlet on rice *katsu-jū* (kot-sue-juu)

rice ball wrapped in seaweed *o-nigiri* (oh-nee-ghee-ree)

roll of rice stuffed with vegetables, cooked egg, etc., wrapped in seaweed *futo-maki* (fuu-toe-mah-kee)

roll of rice with pieces of raw tuna and pickles wrapped in seaweed *nori-maki* (no-ree-mah-kee)

salmon with rice *shake bentō* (shah-kay ben-toe)

seasoned rice wrapped in fried bags of tofu *inari-zushi* (ee-nah-ree-zuu-she)

tempura-fried prawn on rice *ten-jū* (ten-juu)

14

Chinese Restaurants

There are two kinds of Chinese restaurants in Japan, one that is "Chinese" Chinese and one that is "Japanese" Chinese. Restaurants of the first category are known as *chūgoku ryōri-ya* (chuu-go-kuu rio-ree-yah), or Chinese restaurants, while the latter are called *chūka ryōri-ya* (chuu-kah rio-ree-yah), or Chinese-style restaurants.

Chinese-style restaurants, far more numerous, cater to the Japanese on a neighborhood level. Most of these shops are unpretentious and inexpensive, and can be found virtually everywhere. They feature Chinese noodle and rice dishes with various kinds of ingredients and toppings. Their selections are often displayed as plastic replicas in shop windows. Following are some typical dishes:

bean curd with spicy ground meat *mābō-dōfu* (mah-boe-doe-fuu)

cold noodles with meat and vegetables *hiyashi chūka* (he-yah-she chuu-kah)

corn soup *kōn sūpu* (kone suu-puu)

crab with scrambled egg *kani-tama* (kah-nee-tah-mah)

crispy fried noodles with meat and vegetables *katai yaki-soba* (kah-tie yah-kee-so-bah)

egg roll *haru-maki* (hah-rue-mah-kee)

egg soup *tamago sūpu* (tah-mah-go suu-puu)

fried dumplings of minced pork, vegetables, and garlic *gyōza* (g'yoe-zah)

fried noodles *yaki-soba* (yah-kee-so-bah)

fried rice with crab *kani chāhan* (kah-nee chah-hahn)

fried rice with "five ingredients" *gomoku chāhan* (go-moe-kuu chah-hahn)

fried rice with scrambled egg, vegetables, and meat *chāhan* (chah-hahn) fried rice with shrimp *ebi chāhan* (ay-bee chah-hahn)

meat and vegetables on rice *chūka-don* (chuu-kah-doan)

meat dumplings in soup *wantan* (wahn-tahn)

meat dumplings with noodles *wantan men* (wahn-tahn men)

noodles in chicken or pork broth *rāmen* (rah-men)

noodles in curry-flavored broth *karē rāmen* (kah-ray rah-men)

noodles in miso broth *miso rāmen* (me-so rah-men)

noodles in miso broth with butter *batā rāmen* (bah-tah rah-men)

noodles in salty broth *shio rāmen* (she-oh rah-men)

noodles with Chinese pickles *zāsai men* (zah-sie men)

noodles with soybean sprouts *moyashi soba* (moe-yah-she so-bah)

noodles with meat and vegetables *gomoku soba* (go-moe-kuu so-bah)

roast pork with noodles *chāshū men* (chah-shuu men)

shrimp in chili sauce *ebi no chiri sōsu-ni* (ay-bee no chee-ree so-suu-nee)

steamed Chinese dumplings *shūmai* (shuu-my)

stir-fried beef and cabbage *niku to kyabetsu no itame* (nee-kuu toe k'yah-bet-sue no ee-tah-may)

stir-fried beef and vegetables *niku yasai itame* (nee-kuu yah-sie ee-tah-may)

stir-fried pork and green peppers *buta-niku to pīman no itame* (buu-tah-nee-kuu toe pee-mahn no ee-tah-may)

stir-fried vegetables *yasai itame* (yah-sie ee-tah-may)

sweet-and-sour pork *su-buta* (sue-buu-tah)

15

Fugu-ya

GLOBEFISH RESTAURANTS

Fugu-ya (fuu-guu-yah) specialize in globefish (blowfish), probably the most notorious of all Japanese foods. Globefish possess a gland that secretes a highly poisonous substance that is part of their defense mechanism. If this gland is not removed carefully during the preparation process, the poison is released and enters the fish's flesh. The poison is colorless, tasteless, and generally fatal. However, *fugu* chefs receive special training and there is little danger when eating the fish in a licensed shop. *Fugu* is usually cut into very thin slices and eaten as *sashimi* (sah-she-me).

In addition to *fugu-ya,* other high-class restaurants may have *fugu* on their menus. *Fugu* is considered a seasonal dish and most of the latter restaurants offer it only during the winter months. Following are some of the most popular *fugu* dishes:

fugu chiri (fuu-guu chee-ree) globefish and vegetable stew

fugu sashi (fuu-guu sah-she) thinly sliced, raw globefish

fugu zōsui (fuu-guu zoe-sue-e) globefish stew poured over rice

shire zake (she-ray zah-kay) toasted globefish fin served in hot saké

16

Gyūniku-ya
BEEF RESTAURANTS

Gyūniku (g'yuu-nee-kuu) means beef and these beef shops are one of the many types of fast-food restaurants usually found adjoining busy commuter terminals. The specialty in these inexpensive places is *gyū-don* (g'yuu-doan), strips of barbecued beef and leeks on top of a bowl of rice. In some restaurants the beef strips are cooked in an egg batter with leeks. The beef used in *gyūniku-ya* tends to be quite fatty. A side dish of pickled cabbage or radish usually comes with the order.

17

Izaka-ya
PUBS

Among the most popular eating and drinking places in Japan are the *izaka-ya* (ee-zah-kah-yah), often translated as tavern or saloon but more accurately described as a very Japanese-style pub. *Izaka-ya* come in all sizes and shapes. What distinguishes the larger ones is their extensive offering of traditional

Japanese as well as Western dishes, and their waiters and waitresses dressed in traditional clothing. These employees shout out greetings to new arrivals and place all orders by shouting to cooks who acknowledge the orders by shouting back. All of this generally makes for a lively, noisy atmosphere.

Izaka-ya are popular with a wide range of people, from university students to middle-aged office workers. Their popularity is based not only on their working-class prices and extensive menus but also on the typical Japanese atmosphere, including the drinking and crowding that allow patrons to dispense with the strict formal etiquette required during working hours.

Foreign visitors are enthusiastically welcomed at *izaka-ya,* although it is automatically assumed that any foreigner who steps into this conspicuously Japanese atmosphere either speaks some Japanese or is with someone who does. Visitors must be prepared to be seated at community tables, sometimes squeezed in with strangers.

The usual approach at *izaka-ya* is to order a variety of a la carte dishes, varying the selection each visit in order to sample more of the many choices. Most people begin by ordering beer or saké while they look over the menu, and drinks are generally served very quickly no matter how crowded the place might be.

When you are ready to order, just name the dishes you want. Unless you specify that you want more than one dish of a particular item, you will get only one dish, no matter how many people are in your party. In other words, if there are six in your party and you all want *tako su* (tah-koe sue), vinegared octopus, you have to order six *tako su*.

A typical *izaka-ya* has several varieties of food and cooking styles, including seafood, meat, fowl, vegetables, and fruit that either are served raw or fresh, or are grilled, fried, stewed, vinegared, raw, or fresh. Grilled foods may be grilled in butter, *batā-yaki* (bah-tah-yah-kee); with salt, *shio-yaki* (she-oh-yah-kee); with plum sauce, *ume-yaki* (uu-may-yah-kee); with a saké-sweetened soy sauce, *teri-yaki* (tay-ree-yah-kee); or with butter and oil, *okariba-yaki* (oh-kah-ree-bah-yah-kee). Following are some of the grilled things on a typical *izaka-ya* menu:

asparagus wrapped in bacon *asupara bēkon* (ah-sue-pah-rah bay-kone)

Atka mackerel *hokke* (hoke-kay)

boneless chicken breast *sasami* (sah-sah-me)

broiled chicken on skewers *yaki-tori* (yah-kee-toe-ree)

broiled tofu steak with soy sauce and grated radish *tōfu sutēki* (toe-fuu sue-tay-kee)

chicken meatballs *tsukune* (t'sue-kuu-nay)

chicken wing *tebasaki* (tay-bah-sah-kee)

dried cuttlefish *surume* (sue-rue-may)

eggplant broiled with sweet miso paste *nasu dengaku* (nah-sue den-gah-kuu)

fish cake made from grated yam *hanpen* (hahn-pen)

flounder *karei* (kah-ray-e)

garlic *ninniku* (neen-nee-kuu)

green pepper *pīman* (pee-mahn)

grilled clams *yaki-hamaguri* (yah-kee-hah-mah-guu-ree)

grilled eggplant *nasu-yaki* (nah-sue-yah-kee)

grilled tofu *atsu-age* (aht-sue-ah-gay)

herring *nishin* (nee-sheen)

horse mackerel *aji* (ah-jee)

intestine *horumon-yaki* (hoe-rue-moan-yah-kee)

mackerel pike *sanma* (sahn-mah)

potatoes fried in butter *jagaimo batā* (jah-guy-moe bah-tah)

prawn *kuruma-ebi* (kuu-rue-mah-ay-bee)

raw-fish platter *sashimi moriawase* (sah-she-me moe-ree-ah-wah-say)

ray fillet *ei hire* (ay-ee he-ray)

roast beef grilled on a skewer *gyū rōsu kushi-yaki* (g'yuu roe-suu kuu-she-yah-kee)

roast pork *yaki-buta* (yah-kee-buu-tah)

salmon *sake* (sah-kay)

scallop *hotate-gai* (hoe-tah-tay-guy)

shiitake mushroom *shī-take* (she-e-tah-kay)

short-necked clam *asari* (ah-sah-ree)

shrimp *ebi* (ay-bee)

smelt *shishamo* (she-shah-moe)

spare rib *supea ribu* (sue-pay-ah ree-buu)

squid *ika maru-yaki* (ee-kah mah-rue-yah-kee)

squid tentacle *geso* (gay-soe)

Deep-fried foods commonly available at *izaka-ya* include:

cheese rolls *chīzu tsutsumi-age* (chee-zuu t'sue-t'sue-me-ah-gay)

eggplant and cheese *nasu chīzu-age* (nah-sue chee-zuu-ah-gay)

freshwater shrimp *kawa-ebi* (kah-wah-ay-bee)

fried potatoes *poteto furai* (poe-tay-toe fuu-rye)

squid tentacle *geso kara-age* (gay-soe kah-rah-ah-gay)

tofu in light batter *agedashi-dōfu* (ah-gay-dah-she-doe-fuu)

young chicken without batter *waka-tori kara-age* (wah-kah-toe-ree kah-rah-ah-gay)

Stewed and boiled dishes commonly available include:

assorted fish *arani* (ah-rah-nee)

carrots and burdock root *kinpira* (keen-pee-rah)

egg custard with bits of chicken, seafood, and vegetables *chawan-mushi* (chah-wahn-muu-she)

fish cake, eggs, tofu, etc., cooked in stock *oden* (oh-den)

potatoes stewed with pork *niku-jaga* (nee-kuu-jah-gah)

soybean-paste soup *miso-shiru* (me-soe-she-rue)

spinach with dried bonito shavings *o-hitashi* (oh-he-tah-she)

tofu with bits of pork *niku-dōfu* (nee-kuu-doe-fuu)

vegetables with meat bits *ni-komi* (nee-koe-me)

Izaka-ya salads, among their most popular dishes, include the following:

Chinese-style salad (Chinese vegetables and a spicy sauce) *chūka sarada* (chuu-kah sah-rah-dah)

combination salad *nama yasai* (nah-mah yah-sie)

Japanese-style salad (vegetables with sesame and vinegar dressing) *wafū sarada* (wah-fuu sah-rah-dah)

seaweed salad *kaisō sarada* (kie-soh sah-rah-dah)

spring onions *naga negi* (nah-gah nay-ghee)

tuna salad *tsuna sarada* (t'sue-nah sah-rah-dah)

All *izaka-ya* offer a variety of rice and noodle dishes, including many of the following:

rice with broth and green tea *o-chazuke* (oh-chah-zuu-kay)

rice with broth, green tea, and cooked salmon *sake chazuke* (sah-kay chah-zuu kay)

rice with broth, green tea, and dried seaweed *nori chazuke* (no-ree chah-zuu-kay)

rice with broth, green tea, and pickled plum *ume chazuke* (uu-may chah-zuu-kay)

rice with broth, green tea, and spiced cod roe *mentai-ko chazuke* (men-tie-koe chah-zuu-kay)

fried Chinese-style noodles *yaki-soba* (yah-kee-so-bah)

fried *udon* noodles *yaki-udon* (yah-kee-uu-doan)

Snack items available at *izaka-ya* include many of the following:

buttered potatoes *jagaimo batā* (jah-guy-moe bah-tah)

chilled sliced tomatoes *hiyashi tomato* (he-yah-she toe-mah-toe)

chilled tofu garnished with ginger, scallions, and soy sauce *hiya-yakko* (he-yah-yahk-koe)

cucumber with miso paste *moro-kyū* (moe-roe-que)

eel and eggs *una-tama* (uu-nah-tah-mah)

fermented soybeans *nattō* (not-toe)

fish cake with horseradish *ita-wasa* (ee-tah-wah-sah)

french fries *furaido poteto* (fuu-rye-doe poe-tay-toe); *poteto furai* (poe-tay-toe fuu-rye)

fried oysters *kaki furai* (kah-kee fuu-rye)

gingko nut *ginnan* (gheen-nahn)

green soybeans in pods *eda-mame* (eh-dah-mah-may)

pickled vegetables *o-shinko* (oh-sheen-koe)

sweet potato *satsuma-imo* (sot-sue-mah-ee-moe)

Sashimi (sah-she-me), raw fish, is also an *izaka-ya* standby. Common varieties include the following:

abalone *awabi* (ah-wah-bee)

bonito *katsuo-tataki* (kot-sue-oh-tah-tah-kee)

combination plate *sashimi moriawase* (sah-she-me moe-ree-ah-wah-say)

horse mackerel *aji-tataki* (ah-jee-tah-tah-kee)

octopus *tako* (tah-koe)

squid *ika* (ee-kah)

sweet shrimp *ama-ebi* (ah-mah-ay-bee)

tuna *maguro* (mah-guu-roe)

young yellowtail *hamachi* (hah-mah-chee)

18

Kamameshi-ya

"RICE POT" RESTAURANTS

Kama (kah-mah) is a metal cooking pot. *Meshi* (may-she) means boiled rice and by extension food or meal. Together the words form *kamameshi* (kah-mah-may-she), a delicious rice dish. Bits of chicken, crab, shrimp, or other seafood are mixed with chopped bamboo shoots, mushrooms, peas, and other vegetables and stirred into flavored rice in a metal pot. A layer of the main ingredient is added as topping. The dish is then steamed, and the taste of the various ingredients mixes in with the rice, which turns a light brown from the sauces and natural juices of the ingredients. When the rice is cooked, the pot is covered with a wooden lid, then placed in a wooden serving box.

There are more than a dozen *kamameshi* dishes, distinguished by the primary topping. If you are in a *kamameshi* restaurant, just say the name of the main ingredient; in other restaurants where *kamameshi* is on the menu, add the word *meshi* to your order. Following is a list of common types of *kamameshi:*

abalone *awabi* (ah-wah-bee)
bamboo shoots *takenoko* (tah-kay-no-koe)
beef *bifu* (bee-fuu)

chestnut *kuri* (kuu-ree)

chicken *tori* (toe-ree)

clam *asari* (ah-sah-ree)

crab *kani* (kah-nee)

matsutake mushroom *matsu-take* (mot-sue-tah-kay)

oyster *kaki* (kah-kee)

salmon *sake* (sah-kay)

scallop *hotate-gai* (hoe-tah-tay-guy)

shiitake mushroom *shii-take* (she-e-tah-kay)

vegetables, boiled egg bits, and powdered cod meat *sanshoku* (sahn-show-kuu)

vegetables, seafood, and chicken *gomoku* (go-moe-kuu)

Most *kamameshi* shops also serve a number of side dishes, including *yaki-tori* (yah-kee-toe-ree), or barbecued chicken tidbits, and rice soups made with chicken, crab, etc.

19

Kani-ya

CRAB RESTAURANTS

As in many countries, *kani* (kah-nee), crab, is a delicacy in Japan. Specialty crab restaurants feature crab as a main dish, as well as crab in rice and soup dishes. Crab dishes are also available in some Chinese restaurants. Following are some of the more popular crab dishes:

kani chāhan (kah-nee chah-hahn) fried rice with crab

kani meshi (kah-nee may-she) rice and crab steamed in a pot

kani sarada (kah-nee sah-rah-dah) crab salad

kani su (kah-nee sue) vinegared crab

kani tama (kah-nee tah-mah) crab and scrambled egg

20

Kappō-ya
KAPPŌ RESTAURANTS

Kappō (kahp-poe) consists of fresh fish and seasonal vegetables prepared and served in an elegant, traditional setting. *Kappō* restaurants, which tend to be expensive, are usually found in Japanese-style inns called *ryokan* (rio-kahn). Japanese inns have always provided food for their lodgers and today some of the older, more prestigious inns also extend their meal services to the general public. Some of these inns specialize in the style of cooking and serving that is known as *kappō*.

In *kappō* cooking seasonal fish and vegetables are prepared on a "meal of the day" basis in which diners have little or no choice in what they are served. Special requests may be made at the time reservations are made, and additional side dishes may be ordered during meals, however.

Inns following this system depend on their reputations to attract the well-heeled clientele that likes this type of cultural treat. At these restaurants reservations are always required. The cost per person is a flat sum known to the patron from past experience or determined at the time reservations are made. The larger the set charge, the greater the number of dishes served and the higher the quality of the food. It is usually necessary to have reservations made by a knowledgeable Japanese contact.

21

Kissaten
COFFEE SHOPS

The term *kissaten* (keece-sah-ten) covers several types of restaurants, including coffee shops, *kōhī-shoppu* (koe-he-shope-puu), tearooms, and *kanmi-ya* (kahn-me-yah) or *shiruko-ya* (she-rue-koe-yah), traditional Japanese-sweets shops.

Japanese coffee shops range from small places that feature coffee and other soft drinks to large, elaborate shops with extensive menus of both Japanese and Western dishes, plus music of one kind or another. Some coffee shops cater to students and other young people who like jazz and lengthy conversation. Others are patronized by businessmen, shoppers, and dating couples.

There are presently over 161,000 registered coffee shops in all of Japan, approximately one-fifth of which are in the Tokyo metropolitan area. Virtually all office buildings have at least one basement coffee shop, and some have several.

Japanese tearooms do have tea and other drinks but their primary forte is Western-style desserts. Tearooms are not as common as coffee shops, and are usually found in popular shopping districts and around transportation terminals. In Tokyo's Shinjuku area, for example, there are probably over a hundred tearooms.

Kanmi-ya, which means sweets shop, feature Japanese-style desserts, along with various other snack items and soft drinks. These shops are also known as *shiruko-ya.* Most are found in popular shopping areas and near commuter terminals.

A special characteristic of *kissaten,* particularly coffee shops, is that they are primarily meeting places and secondarily restaurants. Many patrons stay for an hour or more, sipping their coffee, juice, etc., and sometimes eating light snack items. As a result, there are no free refills of coffee or other drinks, and prices for single drinks tend to be high by Western standards.

Coffee shops in large hotels are different. These are

full-fledged restaurants with extensive breakfast, lunch, and dinner menus, some with free coffee refills. In a few hotel coffee shops or lounges, coffee is served in small pots that hold two or more cups. If you order a second pot, there is a new charge. Following are drinks commonly found in a Japanese-style coffee shop:

black tea with lemon or milk *kōcha* (koe-chah)

iced tea *aisu tī* (aye-sue tee)

lemon tea *remon tī* (ray-moan tee)

milk tea *miruku tī* (me-rue-kuu tee)

Coca-cola *Kokakōra* (koe-kah-koe-rah)

coffee *kōhī* (koe-he)

American-style (weak) coffee *Amerikan* (ah-may-ree-kahn)

café au lait *kafē o re* (kah-fay oh ray)

cappuccino *kapuchīno* (kah-puu-chee-no)

coffee float (iced coffee with vanilla ice cream) *kōhī furōto* (koe-hee fuu-roe-toe)

iced coffee *aisu kōhī* (aye-sue koe-he)

mocha blend *moka* (moe-kah)

strong blend coffee *burendo* (buu-ren-doe)

Vienna coffee (with whipped cream) *Uinna* (wean-nah)

hot chocolate *kokoa* (koe-koe-ah)

grape drink *gurēpu jūsu* (guu-ray-puu juu-sue)

lemon squash *remon sukasshu* (ray-moan sue-kah-shuu)

orange drink *orenji jūsu* (oh-ren-jee juu-sue)

Pepsi Cola *Pepushikōra* (pep-she koe-rah)

tomato juice *tomato jūsu* (toe-mah-toe juu-sue)

Following are desserts commonly found in a Japanese-style coffee shop:

cheesecake *chīzu kēki* (chee-zuu kay-kee)

chocolate cake *chokorēto kēki* (choe-koe-ray-toe kay-kee)

chocolate sundae with fruit *chokorēto pafe* (choe-koe-ray-toe pah-fay)

egg custard *purin* (puu-reen)

fruit sundae *furūtsu pafe* (fuu-root-sue pah-fay)

ice cream *aisu kurīmu* (aye-sue kuu-ree-muu)

Following are light meals commonly served in a Japanese-style coffee shop:

baked macaroni with ham *hamu guratan* (hah-muu guu-rah-tahn)

baked macaroni with shrimp *ebi guratan* (ay-bee guu-rah-tahn)

baked rice with cheese and seafood *shīfūdo doria* (she-fuu-doe doe-ree-ah)

chicken pilaf *chikin pirafu* (chee-keen pee-rah-fuu)

curried pilaf *karē pirafu* (kah-ray pee-rah-fuu)

egg sandwich *eggu sando* (egg-guu sahn-doe)

ground-beef patty with vegetables *hanbāgu sutēki* (hahn-bah-guu sue-tay-kee)

ham sandwich *hamu sando* (hah-muu sahn-doe)

mixed sandwich *mikkusu sando* (meek-kuu-sue sahn-doe)

morning set (coffee, toast, egg) *mōningu-setto* (moe-neen-guu-set-toe) pizza *piza* (pee-zah)

seafood au gratin *shīfūdo guratan* (she-fuu-doe guu-rah-tahn)

spaghetti with Bolognese meat sauce *supagetti boronēzu* (spa-get-tee boe-roe-nay-zuu)

spaghetti with cream sauce, bacon, and mushrooms *supagetti karubonāra* (spa-get-tee kah-rue-boe-nah-rah)

spaghetti with meat sauce *supagetti mīto sōsu* (spa-get-tee meat-toe soe-sue)

spaghetti with tomato sauce and vegetables *supagetti naporitan* (spa-get-tee nah-poe-ree-tahn)

toast *tōsuto* (toe-sue-toe)

toast with melted cheese *chīzu tōsuto* (chee-zuu toe-sue-toe)

22

Korean-style Yakiniku-ya
BARBECUED-MEAT RESTAURANTS

Yakiniku-ya (yah-kee-nee-kuu-ya) are Korean-style restaurants, and the food served there is often called Korean barbecue. These restaurants feature beef and vegetables barbecued on table grills, along with *kimuchi* (keem-chee), Korea's spicy pickle dish, and various other meat, seafood, and vegetable side dishes. Like Japanese food, Korean cuisine is distinguished by the liberal use of soy sauce, but rather than the natural taste preferred by Japanese, Koreans use copious amounts of hot peppers in their sauces, soups, and cooking broths.

Most meals in *yakiniku-ya* are built around marinated strips of beef that diners barbecue at their own tables. Better restaurants have two grades of beef; *rōsu* (roe-suu), which is sliced from a roast cut, and *jō-rōsu* (joe-roe-suu), a higher grade of roast. Following are other dishes usually found on *yakiniku-ya* menus:

cut of meat with considerable fat *karubi* (kah-rue-bee)

egg soup *tamago sūpu* (tah-mah-go suu-puu)

fresh vegetables *nama yasai-yaki* (nah-mah ya-sie-yah-kee)

heart *hatsu-yaki* (hot-sue-yah-kee)

liver *rebā-yaki* (ray-bah-yah-kee)

meat and vegetable soup *kuppa* (kupe-pah)

minced meat with egg yolk *yukke* (yuke-kay)

mixed vegetables (bean sprouts, radish, spinach) *namuru* (nah-muu-rue)

pickled cucumbers *oi-kimuchi* (oh-ee-keem-chee)

pickled radish *kakuteki* (kah-kuu-tay-kee)

pickled white cabbage *kimuchi* (keem-chee)

raw liver *rebā sashi* (ray-bah sah-she)

raw squid *ika sashi* (ee-kah sah-she)

seaweed soup *wakame sūpu* (wah-kah-may suu-puu)

soup with mixed vegetables and boiled rice *bibimba* (bee-beem-bah)

squid *ika-yaki* (ee-kah-yah-kee)

tongue *tan-yaki* (tahn-yah-kee)

tripe *mino-yaki* (me-no-yah-kee)

In Korean-style restaurants, a set lunch is called *yaki-niku bentō* (yah-kee-nee-kuu ben-toe), and a set dinner is *yaki-niku teishoku* (yah-kee-nee-kuu tay-show-kuu). Most restaurants have three or more set courses that vary from lunches to complete meals.

23

Koryōri-ya
"SMALL FOOD" RESTAURANTS

Koryōri-ya (koe-rio-ree-yah) is a generic term that covers a variety of restaurants serving *koryōri,* literally small food, or what is usually thought of as Japanese food—fish, other seafood, chicken, *tōfu,* and all sorts of vegetables deep-fried, grilled, or boiled, served a la carte, and invariably accompanied by beer or saké.

The *koryōri-ya* are something like pubs or taverns in that people patronize them after work to both eat and drink in a very informal atmosphere. They usually have stools around a bar, some tables, and often two or more semiprivate rooms with tatami floors for small groups. The decor and service are traditional Japanese, and patrons tend to become regulars at favorite places. Customers generally stay for two or more hours, eating, drinking, and talking in a high-spirited manner. Following are some typical a la carte dishes on *koryōri-ya* menus:

aji-tataki (ah-jee-tah-tah-kee) Pompano fish *sashimi*,
  cut into tiny pieces but otherwise intact, with the
  head and tail included, on a bed of seaweed or sliced
  radish.

chawan-mushi (chah-wahn-muu-she) Immediately popular with most foreign visitors, this is a dinner custard
  containing bits of chicken, shrimp, mushrooms,
  gingko nuts, pea pods, and pieces of fish cake. It is
  prepared in a covered cup or small bowl.

chiri-mushi (chee-ree-muu-she) A fillet of either tilefish
  or sea bream (red snapper) and vegetables steamed
  in a bowl. Served with a soy-based sauce made with
  lemon juice, grated radish, and leeks.

chiri-nabe (chee-ree-nah-bay) Leeks, tofu, cabbage,
  mushrooms, and fish (usually cod or angler) boiled
  in bouillon in an earthenware pot at the table. A
  spicy sauce is used as a dip.

dengaku (den-gah-kuu) The odd name of this dish
  comes from an ancient folk drama and refers to a
  food popular with patrons viewing *dengaku* plays. It
  consists of blocks of tofu or *konnyaku* (kone-yah-kuu),
  a gelatin made from devil's-tongue root, skewered on
  bamboo sticks, coated with miso sauce, and broiled
  over charcoal. Unskewered eggplant, potatoes, and
  radish may also be prepared in this manner.

dobin-mushi (doe-bean-muu-she) Mushrooms, sliced or
  whole, bits of chicken or shrimp, plus gingko nuts
  and other vegetables boiled in a soup stock made of
  fish bouillon that has been seasoned with saké and
  mirin (me-reen), a sweet cooking wine. The dish,
  most popular in the fall and early winter, is served

in a small, handled teapot. Diners use the teapot lid or a separate saucer as a plate.

dote-nabe (doe-tay-nah-bay) A wonderful winter specialty usually prepared at the diner's table, this is a casserole of oysters, tofu, carrots, leeks, and chrysanthemum leaves seasoned with sweetened miso paste. Aficionados use a beaten raw egg on the side as a dip.

eda-mame (eh-dah-mah-may) Soybeans still in their green pods, boiled and salted, served as an appetizer. The pods are tough and not eaten.

hiya-yakko (he-yah-yahk-koe) A block of tofu, served cold, with grated ginger, chopped leeks, and usually a small chunk of boiled spinach on the side as a garnish. The tofu is dipped in soy sauce.

ita-wasa (ee-tah-wah-sah) Most first-time visitors to Japan are taken aback by this dish, which is eaten more for its health benefits than its bland taste. It consists of small slices of the fish cake known as *kamaboko* (kah-mah-boe-koe), served with soy sauce and horseradish, and is usually eaten at the beginning of a meal.

miso-shiru (me-so-she-rue) Japan's most popular soup is made with miso and a fish or seaweed bouillon stock, and usually contains such things as small chunks of tofu, pieces of kelp or other seaweed, and other vegetables.

mizu-taki (mee-zuu-tah-kee) Prepared at your table in a large pot, this dish features pieces of boneless chicken, leeks, tofu, Chinese cabbage, and gelatin noodles called *shirataki* (she-rah-tah-kee), boiled in a stock flavored with seaweed and dried fish shavings. A spicy sauce is served on the side as a dip.

nama yasai (nah-mah yah-sie) A salad usually including tomatoes, asparagus, lettuce, cucumber, onion, hard-boiled egg, and a piece of fruit.

oden (oh-den) Another dish that owes its name to an ancient folk drama, *oden* is a kind of stew consisting of fish cake, tofu, radish, seaweed, octopus, and other ingredients boiled together in a pot of fish bouillon. Hot mustard is usually served on the side. The dish is especially popular in winter.

o-hitashi (oh-he-tah-she) A small bowl of boiled spinach seasoned with soy sauce and topped with shavings of dried bonito. Some restaurants use a sprinkling of sesame seeds instead of bonito shavings as a topping.

sakana teri-yaki (sah-kah-nah tay-ree-yah-kee) A piece of mackerel or yellowtail coated in soy sauce, saké, sugar, and *mirin,* and then broiled. A stick of pickled ginger is usually served with the dish.

sansai nitsuke (sahn-sie neet-sue-kay) A popular hors d'oeuvre consisting of a small mound of mountain fern that has been boiled in a fish bouillon seasoned with soy sauce and *mirin.*

sazae tsubo-yaki (sah-zie t'sue-boe-yah-kee) Chopped wreath-shell meat, boiled in broth flavored with saké and soy sauce, then replaced in the shell and served on a small platter, sometimes on a bed of salt.

shio-yaki (she-oh-yah-kee) A small fish coated in salt and broiled until the skin is slightly charred. Fish most often prepared in this manner include *ayu* (ah-yuu), a freshwater trout; *tai* (tie), sea bream or red snapper; and *kamasu* (kah-mah-sue), pike.

suno-mono (sue-no-moe-no) A vegetable or raw-fish appetizer served in a vinegar dressing.

tamago-yaki (tah-mah-go-yah-kee) An omelette, seasoned
   with soy sauce and sweet wine, cooked in layers,
   then rolled up and sliced into pieces. In some
   restaurants this dish is called *dashi-maki* (dah-she-
   mah-kee).

tori kara-age (toe-ree kah-rah-ah-gay) Chunks of chicken,
   salted and deep-fried, usually served with small
   pieces of vegetable and a slice of lemon.

yaki-hamaguri (yah-kee-hah-mah-guu-ree) Broiled clams
   in the shell, served with salt and lemon.

yaki-tori (yah-kee-toe-ree) This popular dish consists of
   small chunks of chicken, along with green peppers,
   leeks, etc., skewered, seasoned with soy sauce or salt,
   and charcoal broiled.

yasai nitsuke (yah-sie neet-sue-kay) A bowl of seasonal
   vegetables and squares of *konnyaku* in a stock seasoned with soy sauce, salt, and sugar.

yu-dōfu (yuu-doe-fuu) Squares of boiled tofu dipped
   into a mixture of soy sauce, dried bonito flakes,
   grated ginger, and leeks.

24

Kushiage-ya

"SKEWER DEEP-FRY" RESTAURANTS

Another popular cooking
style in Japan is *kushi-age* (kuu-she-ah-gay), foods cut into
small pieces, breaded, skewered, and deep-fried. *Kushi*
(kuu-she) means skewer and *age* (ah-gay) means deep-

fry. There are specialty *kushi-age* restaurants, and *kushi-age* items are also served in some *tonkatsu* restaurants, pubs, and other drinking places. For most diners *kushi-age* foods are side or snack dishes that go with drinking, so *kushi-age* restaurants generally look and sound very much like pubs. *Kushi-age* can be ordered a la carte or as a combination platter, *kushi-age kōsu* (kuu-she-ah-gay koe-sue). Among the things commonly cooked *kushi-age* style are:

asparagus *asuparagasu* (ahss-pah-rah-gah-sue)

bean curd *tōfu* (toe-fuu)

beef *bīfu* (bee-fuu)

boneless chicken breast *sasami-maki* (sah-sah-me-mah-kee)

cheese *chīzu* (chee-zuu)

devil's-tongue gelatin *konnyaku* (kone-yah-kuu)

eggplant *nasu* (nah-sue)

fish cake *tsumire* (t'sue-me-ray)

gingko nuts *ginnan* (gheen-nahn)

green pepper *pīman* (pee-mahn)

green pepper stuffed with ground meat *pīman niku-zume* (pee-mahn nee-kuu-zuu-may)

lotus root *hasu* (hah-sue)

okra *okura* (oh-kuu-rah)

pork *buta* (buu-tah)

quail eggs *uzura tamago* (uu-zuu-rah tah-mah-go)

scallops *hotate-gai* (hoe-tah-tay-guy)

shiitake mushroom *shī-take* (she-e-tah-kay)

shrimp *ebi* (ay-bee)
squid *ika* (ee-kah)
squid tentacle *geso* (gay-so)

25

Kyōdo Ryōri-ya

REGIONAL COUNTRY-STYLE RESTAURANTS

Kyōdo (k'yoe-doe) means one's birthplace or a rural area and in this instance refers to restaurants that feature country-style cooking, usually specializing in one specific style of regional cooking. Fresh fish and vegetables are brought from local regions on a regular and sometimes daily basis.

Individual regional restaurants distinguish themselves by promoting their specialty, things like the oyster dishes of Hiroshima and the salmon dishes of Hokkaido.

26

Menrui-ya

NOODLE SHOPS

At *menrui-ya* (men-rue-ee-yah), noodle shops, diners have their choice of a wide variety of noodle dishes in both Japanese and Chinese style. The five kinds of Japanese noodles include *soba* (so-bah), which are long and brownish-gray and made from buckwheat flour; *udon* (uu-doan), long, white noodles made from wheat flour; *hiya-mugi* (he-yah-muu-ghee), long, white noodles made from wheat flour and served cold in the summer; *sōmen* (so-men), very thin, very long, white noodles made from wheat and usually served in cold water; and *himo-kawa* (he-moe-kah-wah), long, flat noodles made from wheat, and called *kishi men* (kee-she men) in some areas.

Popular *soba* dishes are described in Chapter 41. Other Japanese noodle dishes, available at *soba-ya, udon-ya, koryōri-ya,* and other restaurants include the following:

ankake udon (ahn-kah-kay uu-doan) A winter dish made with *udon* noodles. Soup stock is made from fish bouillon seasoned with soy sauce. Ingredients include fish cake, mushrooms, bamboo shoots, and spinach.

chikara udon (chee-kah-rah uu-doan) *Udon* noodles in a fish broth, with pieces of the glutinous rice cake called *mochi* (moe-chee), fish cake, spinach, and sometimes fried bits of batter.

himo-kawa (he-moe-kah-wah) Flat noodles in a fish broth, with slices of fish cake, shaved bonito, bits of spinach, and pieces of fried tofu.

hiya-mugi (he-yah-muu-ghee) A summer dish consisting of long, white noodles served in iced water, along with a few slices of cucumber, tomato, sometimes fruit, and a soy-based dip. A small side dish of chopped leeks and pickled vegetables is included.

kamo nanban (kah-moe nahn-bahn) Either *soba* or *udon*
noodles in soy-seasoned fish bouillon, with chunks of
duck or chicken and sliced leeks.

karē nanban (kah-ray nahn-bahn) *Udon* noodles and
pieces of beef or pork in a curry-flavored soup.

kishi zaru (kee-she zah-rue) *Kishi men* noodles with strips
of dried seaweed on top, served cold with a soy dip
and condiments on the side.

kitsune udon (keet-sue-nay uu-doan) *Udon* noodles with
pieces of leeks and fried tofu, served in a soy-
seasoned fish broth. There is usually a side dish of
chopped raw leeks.

miso nikomi udon (me-soe nee-koe-me uu-doan) A winter
dish of *udon* noodles boiled in a thick miso-and-fish
broth, along with large pieces of leeks, mushrooms,
sometimes gelatin noodles, and a piece of *fu* (fuu), a
fluffy wheat gluten. Served in an earthenware pot.

nabe-yaki udon (nah-bay-yah-kee uu-doan) A winter dish
of *udon* noodles in soy-seasoned fish broth, with
pieces of bamboo shoots, mushrooms, spinach, fish
cake, and wheat gluten on top. Some shops add half
of a hardboiled egg and a tempura-fried shrimp.
Served in a casserole dish.

nameko udon (nah-may-koe uu-doan) *Udon* noodles in a
soy-seasoned fish broth, with small mushrooms called
nameko, spinach, dried seaweed, and grated radish.

niku nanban (nee-kuu nahn-bahn) *Soba* or *udon* noodles
in a soy-and-fish bouillon, with thin slices or chunks
of pork and leeks.

sōmen (so-men) A summer dish of thin, white noodles
served in cold or iced water, with pieces of cucumber, tomato, a cherry, and other ingredients.

tamago toji (tah-mah-go toe-jee) *Udon* noodles in a soy-and-fish bouillon, with a boiled egg, fish cake, and dried seaweed. Sliced leeks and grated horseradish are condiments.

tanuki udon (tah-nuu-kee uu-doan) *Udon* noodles in a soy-and-fish bouillon, with fried bits of batter, slices of fish cake, and spinach.

tenpura udon (ten-puu-rah uu-doan) One or two tempura-fried shrimp and spinach on top of *udon* noodles in a soy-and-fish bouillon.

The Chinese noodle is made from a mixture of wheat flour, eggs, salt, and a special mineral water. Popular Chinese-style noodle dishes include the following:

chanpon (chahn-pone) Chinese noodles in a salt-seasoned bouillon, with pieces of pork, Chinese cabbage, bean sprouts, bamboo shoots, and wood ear (tree fungus) precooked in a thick sauce that serves as a topping.

chāshū men (chah-shuu men) Chinese noodles in a soy-and-pork bouillon, with pieces of sliced pork, spinach, and diced leeks.

gomoku soba (go-moe-kuu so-bah) Chinese noodles in a pork-flavored broth, with at least five additional ingredients, including such things as sliced ham, hard-boiled egg, fish cake, Chinese cabbage, bamboo shoots, pork, and spinach.

hiyashi chūka (he-yah-she chuu-kah) A summer dish of Chinese noodles served cold on a plate, covered with a sauce made of sesame-seed oil, vinegar, soy sauce, sugar and red pepper, and topped with strips of pickled ginger, fish cake, cucumber, and ham. Also called *hiyashi soba* and *hiyashi rāmen.*

kanton men (kahn-tone men) Chinese noodles in a pork stock, with pieces of pork, cabbage, bamboo shoots, carrots, pea pods, etc., precooked in a thick sauce that is poured over the noodles.

miso rāmen (me-so rah-men) Chinese noodles in a miso broth, with pieces of pork, bean sprouts, and spinach.

moyashi soba (moe-yah-she so-bah) Chinese noodles in a pork broth, with sautéed bamboo shoots, carrot strips, and *moyashi,* bean sprouts.

rāmen (rah-men) The most popular and cheapest of all Chinese-style noodle dishes, *rāmen* consists of Chinese noodles in a soy-and-pork broth, with slices of pork or ham, spinach, and leeks.

tan men (tahn men) Chinese noodles in a pork broth, with bits of pork or ham, carrots, bamboo shoots, Chinese cabbage, and mushrooms.

wantan men (wahn-tahn men) Chinese noodles in a soy broth, with dumplings filled with ground pork and leeks, usually with two or three other items like fish cake, bamboo, and spinach.

27

Nabemono-ya
"POT THINGS" RESTAURANTS

One of the most popular and interesting categories of Japanese cuisine, *nabe-mono* (nah-bay-moe-no), which literally means "pot thing," refers to stewlike dishes that are cooked in pots and generally eaten in winter. The best-known "pot dishes" are sukiyaki and *shabu-shabu,* but these are regarded as special varieties of *nabe-mono* and treated separately.

Nabe-mono dishes are made with familiar ingredients: seafood, vegetables, chicken, meat, noodles, tofu, and so on. Their special attraction is the combination of these things quickly stewed together and enhanced by special stocks and sauces. While the quick stewing leaves much of the natural taste and texture of the ingredients intact, the juices of the ingredients intermingle during the meal, gradually changing the taste of the cooking stock.

Some larger *nabe-mono* restaurants have tables with their own gas burners, allowing diners to prepare things at their own pace. Restaurant employees will assist beginners preparing food the *nabe* way. Smaller restaurants offering *nabe-mono* prepare orders in their kitchens and serve them in bowls. Many people top off a *nabe-mono* meal by pouring a cup or more of broth over a bowl of rice.

A favorite *nabe* dish among many first-time visitors to Japan is *mizu-taki* (me-zuu-tah-kee), chicken, tofu, and vegetables cooked at the table in a clear broth, and eaten after being dipped into a mixture of soy sauce, peanut oil, and other ingredients. The standard dish of Japan's huge sumo wrestlers is a variety of *nabe-mono* called *chanko-nabe* (chahn-koe nah-bay), which contains up to a dozen or so of the ingredients used in other *nabe* dishes. Following are other popular *nabe* dishes:

angler-fish stew *ankō-nabe* (ahn-koe-nah-bay)

cod and vegetable stew *tara-nabe* (tah-rah-nah-bay)

duck and vegetable stew *kamo-nabe* (kah-moe-nah-bay)

fish and vegetable stew *chiri-nabe* (chee-ree-nah-bay)

loach (small freshwater fish), burdock root, and egg stew *yanagawa-nabe* (yah-nah-gah-wah-nah-bay)

noodles and fish stew *udon-suki* (uu-doan-ski)

oyster and vegetable stew with miso *dote-nabe* (doe-tay-nah-bay)

salmon and vegetable stew with miso and butter *Ishikari-nabe* (ee-she-kah-ree-nah-bay)

seafood, chicken, and vegetable stew *yose-nabe* (yoe-say-nah-bay)

28

Nomi-ya

NEIGHBORHOOD PUBS

Nomi-ya (no-me-yah), which means drinking place, might be referred to as Japan's neighborhood bar. The typical *nomi-ya* is small, sometimes just a tiny hole-in-the-wall with a small bar and four to six stools. These places are primarily vendors of beer and saké but also serve a variety of fish and vegetable dishes.

Nomi-ya are often identified by *aka-chōchin,* large, red-paper lanterns hanging outside their front doors. The lanterns serve both to signify a drinking and eating place and to give the name of the shop, which is inscribed on the lantern in large characters. In fact, these shops are also called *aka-chōchin.*

Dishes served in *nomi-ya* are generally those served by other Japanese-style restaurants. Following are some typical *nomi-ya* dishes:

hi-mono (he-moe-no) large pieces of dried fish (flounder, horse mackerel, pike, etc.) broiled, and served with grated radish as a garnish

ika shōga-yaki (ee-kah show-gah-yah-kee) grilled pieces of squid seasoned with soy sauce, grated ginger, and garlic

kinpira (keen-pee-rah) strips of fried burdock root and carrot, seasoned with sweetened soy sauce and red pepper

nattō (not-toe) Made of fermented soybeans, *natto* is a true test of one's culinary courage. It has a strong smell and a gooey texture that many people, even some Japanese, find unpleasant. In *nomi-ya* it is generally seasoned with soy sauce and leeks, and may be sprinkled with dried seaweed. Some aficionados like a raw quail egg poured over the dish.

sui-mono (sue-e-moe-no) soup usually made from a clear fish or seaweed bouillon, lightly seasoned with soy sauce, saké, and salt, and containing things like tofu, fish cake, etc.

tatsuta age (tot-sue-tah ah-gay) small pieces of chicken or fish, marinated in saké and soy sauce, and deep-fried.

29

Ochazuke-ya

"TEA'D RICE" RESTAURANTS

O-chazuke (oh-chah-zuu-kay) is a dish made by pouring green tea, cooking stock, or fish broth over a bowl of cooked white rice, and then adding bits of seaweed, pickles, or fish on top. There are several kinds of *o-chazuke,* depending on the topping:

pickles *tsuke-mono chazuke* (t'sue-kay-moe-no chah-zuu-kay)
salted salmon *sake chazuke* (sah-kay chah-zuu-kay)
sea bream *tai chazuke* (tie chah-zuu-kay)
seaweed *nori chazuke* (no-ree chah-zuu-kay)

This popular food can be eaten at a *shokudō, nomi-ya, sunakku,* or at an *ochazuke-ya* near a commuter terminal. Some fans of *o-chazuke* stir in a dab of hot *wasabi* (wah-sah-bee), horseradish, to spice the dish up.

30

Oden-ya

"JAPANESE STEW" RESTAURANTS

Among the more picturesque sights in Japan's nighttime entertainment areas are

street booths or one-man carts serving *oden* (oh-den), a
Japanese stew that is especially popular in winter.
Chunks of fish cake, tofu, eggs, Japanese radish, and
other ingredients are boiled in fish bouillon and left sim-
mering, sometimes for hours. A hot mustard is also
usually available.

In *oden* shops where you sit at a counter and at street
carts or booths you can pick the individual items you
want. If you do not specify what you want, you are
served an assortment of items. *Oden* is also on the menu
of other Japanese restaurants, particularly *nomi-ya*
(no-me-yah) because its slightly salty taste encourages
drinking. You can order *oden* as a set meal, *oden teishoku*
(oh-den tay-show-kuu), which includes soup, rice, and
pickles. *Oden moriawase* (oh-den moe-ree-ah-wah-say) is
a selection of ingredients without the soup, rice, and
pickles. Following are some of the main ingredients in
oden:

   burdock root *gobō* (go-boe)
   burdock root wrapped in fish cake *gobō-maki* (go-boe-
      mah-kee)
   cabbage roll filled with burdock root *rōru kyabetsu* (roe-
      rue k'yah-bet-sue)
   devil's-tongue gelatin *konnyaku* (kone-yah-kuu)
   fish cake balls *bōru dango* (boe-rue dahn-go)
   fish cake balls made from sardine *tsumire* (t'sue-me-ray)
   fish cake made from shark *suji* (sue-jee)
   fish cake made with yam *hanpen* (hahn-pen)

fish cake shaped like a tube *chikuwa* (chee-kuu-wah)

fried tofu bag filled with chopped vegetables *fukuro* (fuu-kuu-roe)

hard-boiled egg *tamago* (tah-mah-go)

Japanese radish *daikon* (die-kone)

kelp sheets rolled and tied in knots *konbu* (kone-buu)

noodles of devil's-tongue gelatin *shirataki* (she-rah-tah-kee)

octopus on skewers *tako-gushi* (tah-koe-guu-she)

quail eggs *uzura tamago* (uu-zuu-rah tah-mah-go)

squid *ika* (ee-kah)

tofu *yaki-dōfu* (yah-kee-doe-fuu)

tofu patties fried with bits of vegetables *ganmodoki* (gahn-moe-doe-kee)

31

Okonomiyaki-ya

"JAPANESE QUICHE" RESTAURANTS

Another festival and street favorite is *okonomi-yaki* (oh-koe-no-me-yah-kee), often described as a pancake, but I call it "Japanese quiche." It starts out as a thick batter into which chopped vegetables, seafood, meat, and egg are added. The mixture is then spread on a grill and fried like a pancake. Many diners dip the bite-size pieces into a sauce before eating.

In better shops the *okonomi-yaki* are thick enough to

make a meal. Those made by many street vendors are very thin, more a snack than a meal. Specialty shops featuring this dish also usually serve omelettes and *yaki-soba* (yah-kee-so-bah), fried noodles.

Okonomi-yaki ingredients include diced beef, clams, corn, octopus, oysters, shrimp, squid, and various vegetables. Any of these can serve as the chief ingredient of *okonomi-yaki:*

bifu-ten (bee-fuu-ten) made with chopped beef
buta-ten (buu-tah-ten) made with chopped pork
ebi-ten (ay-bee-ten) made with shrimp
ika-ten (ee-kah-ten) made with chopped squid
kaki-ten (kah-kee-ten) made with oysters
modan-yaki (moe-dahn-yah-kee) served with a fried egg

32

Onigiri-ya
RICE-BALL STANDS

O-nigiri (oh-nee-ghee-ree) is the original "sandwich" of Japan, created centuries ago by chefs of the imperial court in Kyoto for court members to take on picnics. The food consists of triangles or balls of rice, wrapped in strips of dried seaweed, with pieces of pickled plum, salted salmon, or codfish eggs inside the rice.

Onigiri-ya are not restaurants in the usual sense of the word but rather shops or stands where these rice sandwiches are sold as takeout food. Many Japanese-style restaurants also have *o-nigiri*, which usually comes in a set of three with a bowl of soup.

33

Rice Dishes

Boiled white rice, *gohan* (go-hahn), which also means meal or food, remains a basic part of the Japanese diet, particularly for older people, who view it the way Westerners do bread or potatoes.

For centuries rice has been a vital part of the Japanese diet, to the point that it has played a key role in the spiritual life of the country and is credited with being a primary factor in the molding of Japanese culture and character. Thus, it is not surprising that the Japanese have developed dozens of dishes to help make rice more appetizing and nutritious. Here are some of the most common rice dishes, along with the types of restaurants where they are usually available:

> *chāhan* (chah-hahn) Rice fried with chopped onions, cooked egg, fish cake, peas, with bits of chicken, crab, pork, or beef. Some restaurants add two or three boiled shrimp. *Shokudō* and Chinese restaurants.

chūka donburi (chuu-kah doan-buu-ree) A plate or bowl of rice covered with a mixture containing pieces of pork, Chinese cabbage, bamboo shoots, pea pods, etc. The ingredients vary with the restaurant. *Shokudō* and Chinese restaurants.

gomoku meshi (go-moe-kuu may-she) Pieces of chicken, vegetables, and fried tofu served over a plate of rice. *Shokudō* and Chinese restaurants.

gyū-don (g'yuu-doan) Thinly sliced strips of beef cooked sukiyaki-style on top of a bowl of rice. A bit of the sauce the meat is cooked in is poured on the rice to add flavor. Specialty *gyū-don* shops and *shokudō*. This is a cheaper version of *niku-don* (nee-kuu-doan), which follows.

hayashi raisu (hah-yah-she rye-sue) A brown gravy containing pieces of beef and onion poured over a plate of rice. Usually eaten with slices of pickled radish. *Shokudō* and Japanese-style restaurants.

karē raisu (kah-ray rye-sue) A curry-flavored stew containing small chunks of beef or pork, along with potatoes and onions, poured over a plate of rice. Tiny pieces of red, Indian-style pickles are served on the side. *Shokudō, soba* and *udon* shops, and other Japanese restaurants.

katsu-don (kot-sue-doan) A breaded pork cutlet cooked with egg, sliced onions, etc., served on a bowl of rice. *Shokudō* and noodle shops.

kuri gohan (kuu-ree go-hahn) Rice cooked with chestnuts. Japanese-style restaurants, *shokudō,* and *ryōtei.*

niku-don (nee-kuu-doan) An individual serving of suki-yaki, composed of slices of beef, onions, leeks, tofu, and gelatin noodles cooked in a sweetened soy-based stock and placed neatly on a bowl of rice. Pickled vegetables are served on the side. *Shokudō* and noodle shops.

omu raisu (oh-muu rye-sue) A mound of rice mixed with tomato sauce, bits of pork or chicken, and wrapped in a plain egg omelette. Usually eaten with ketchup. *Shokudō* and some noodle shops.

oyako donburi (oh-yah-koe doan-buu-ree) Pieces of chicken and onions cooked in egg, garnished with shredded seaweed, and served on a bowl of rice, with pickled vegetables on the side. *Shokudō* and noodle shops.

sekihan (say-kee-hahn) Rice cooked with red beans. Japanese-style restaurants. This dish is frequently eaten on festive occasions.

tamago donburi (tah-mah-go doan-buu-ree) Chopped onions cooked in egg, garnished with shredded seaweed, and served on a bowl of rice. A small, round slice of fish cake often tops the dish. *Shokudō* and noodle shops.

ten-don (ten-doan) One or two pieces of tempura-fried shrimp, dipped in a soy broth, and served on a bowl of rice. A dash of the broth is usually poured over the top of the rice. *Shokudō* and noodle shops.

tonkatsu raisu (tone-kot-sue rye-sue) A breaded, deep-fried pork cutlet on a bowl of rice. Pickles usually accompany the dish. *Shokudō* and other Japanese-style restaurants.

unagi donburi (uu-nah-ghee doan-buu-ree) Pieces of broiled eel, brushed with a sweetened soy sauce, served on a bowl of rice, with pickles on the side. Some Japanese-style restaurants and larger *shokuji-dokoro*.

unajū (uu-nah-juu) Pieces of broiled eel served over rice

in a lacquered box. *Unagi-ya,* larger Japanese-style restaurants, and *ryōtei.*

34

Robatayaki-ya
GRILL RESTAURANTS

Robata-yaki (roe-bah-tah-yah-kee) means fireside cooking, and refers to cooking on charcoal grills, whereas many of the dishes in *izaka-ya* pubs are deep-fried. The *ro-bata* style of cooking is an adaptation of the traditional farmhouse fireplace in a combination kitchen-living room, where most of the cooking was done and where family members gathered for meals and socializing. Many *robatayaki-ya* restaurants are designed and decorated to reflect the rustic flavor of a typical large farmhouse, and a visit here can be a true cultural experience.

Following are the main categories of grilled food served in *robatayaki-ya:*

kara-yaki (kah-rah-yah-kee) shellfish baked in the shells
yaki-niku (yah-kee-nee-kuu) grilled meat
yaki-onigiri (yah-kee-oh-nee-ghee-ree) grilled rice balls
yaki-tori (yah-kee-toe-ree) grilled skewered chicken
yaki-yasai (yah-kee-yah-sie) grilled vegetables
yaki-zakana (yah-kee-zah-kah-nah) grilled fish

35

Ryōtei
INN RESTAURANTS

The *ryōtei* (rio-tay) is the classic upper-class restaurant featuring an elegant meal served in a traditional setting, a Japanese-style building usually with a landscaped garden. Most of these places, which look more like private homes or inns than public restaurants, are located in or near geisha districts or on quiet back streets near major shopping or business districts. Generally these restaurants require reservations, and some have strict policies of never accepting unknown customers.

Some *ryōtei* specialize in *kaiseki* (kie-say-kee) cuisine, small, delicate portions of traditional foods. This style of cooking was originated by Buddhist priests and then refined by tea masters serving guests at tea ceremonies. A *kaiseki* meal consists of a dozen or more dishes designed to give diners a taste of many delicacies. Uninitiated visitors who are not aware of the traditions or purpose of *kaiseki* dining keep waiting for the main dish and are quite surprised when fruit and tea are served, signifying the end of the meal.

Some *ryōtei* restaurants, particularly in the Kyoto-Osaka area, specialize in a type of cooking that originated in Kyoto, which was the capital of Japan from 794 to 1868. This cooking is appropriately known as *Kyō ryōri* (k'yoe rio-ree), or Kyoto food, and is characterized by even more refinement and subtlety than what is found in other Japanese cooking styles.

Ryōtei are significantly more expensive than ordinary restaurants. Ordering is by set courses that feature seasonal vegetables and seafood. *Ryōtei* dishes can be raw, dried, pickled, deep-fried, or broiled. The variety of dishes depends on the course. The more expensive the course, the larger the variety of dishes. A typical course has between eight and a dozen dishes, including rice and fruit at the end of the meal. Most visitors wanting the *ryōtei* experience have their reservations made by Japanese contacts, and more often than not are accompanied by Japanese guides or friends.

36

Traditional Drinks

Japan's traditional alcoholic drinks include the well-known saké, often referred to as *o-sake* (oh-sah-kay), *shōchū* (show-chuu), *umeshu* (uu-may-shuu), and *o-toso* (toe-so). Saké is a white wine made from fermented rice. *Shōchū* is a powerful distilled liquor made from potatoes, rice, etc. It was originally regarded as a drink for blue-collar workers, but in the 1970s its image changed and it became acceptable as Japan's answer to vodka. *Umeshu* is plum or apricot wine. *O-toso* is a mixture of saké, *mirin,* and herbs, and is generally drunk at New Year's to drive evil spirits away.

The main Japanese drink is, of course, saké, which has been made since the dawn of Japanese culture, first as a sacramental drink for Shinto religious ceremonies. Saké still has a semisacred image to the Japanese, and is used to mark all kinds of official occasions, from marriages to the signing of business contracts.

Saké is made in many places in Japan, with some areas having been famous for centuries for the special quality of their product, which is greatly affected by the weather, water, and rice. Alcoholic content is about 32 proof. The lower you go in the vat, the higher the alcoholic content.

Saké does not improve with age. The quality may vary slightly from one year to the next because of the weather or other factors, but the difference is extremely small. There is no such thing as a vintage year for saké.

All saké is graded by government inspectors and given a rank based on taste, color, and aroma.

tokkyū-shu (toke-yuu-shuu) special grade
ikkyū-shu (eek-yuu-shuu) first grade
nikkyū-shu (neek-yuu-shuu) second grade

The first two grades must pass the government's test, and producers must pay a high tax on them.

Saké can be drunk hot, warm, or chilled, but most aficionados prefer it warmed because the heat enhances the aroma, taste, and effect. It is served (and heated) in small ceramic vases called *tokkuri* (toke-kuu-ree), and usually drunk from small cups called *sakazuki* (sah-kah-zuu-kee). Just as beer goes better with some foods, saké complements many Japanese dishes, particularly salty dishes and bland foods like tofu.

Only a genuine *tsū*, or expert, can discern the difference between the various saké brands and grades. If you are given a choice, choose any well-known brand and you will be guaranteed a top-grade saké. There are some 2,600 saké brewers in Japan, with around 4,000 local and national brands. Top brands include Gekkeikan (gake-kay-kahn), Haku Tsuru (hah-kuu t'sue-rue), and Ozeki (oh-zay-kee). The Gekkeikan brewery has been in business since 1637.

To order one *tokkuri* of saké, say *O-sake ippon!* (oh-sah-kay ee-pone). For two bottles, say *O-sake nihon!* (oh-sah-kay nee-hone).

37

Shabushabu-ya
SHABU-SHABU RESTAURANTS

While sukiyaki may be better known among foreign visitors to Japan, many people prefer *shabu-shabu* (shah-buu-shah-buu), a dish of sliced beef and vegetables cooked at the table. The chief difference between it and sukiyaki is that in *shabu-shabu* very thin slices of beef are boiled quickly, in four to six seconds, in a clear stock, as opposed to being cooked for several minutes in a thick, sweetened, soy-based sauce. The usual process is for the diners themselves to submerge each piece of beef in the stock and hold it for the required few seconds. In the meantime, leeks, tofu, Chinese cabbage, and other vegetables are put in the pot to simmer for longer periods. Diners also generally have the option of adding a larger variety of vegetables to the pot. This extra side dish is called *yasai moriawase* (yah-sie moe-ree-ah-wah-say), which more or less means vegetable sampler.

Shabu-shabu diners have two choices of dips, one made of lemon juice and grated radish and one made of soybean paste, sesame seeds, and soy sauce.

38

Shōjin Ryōri-ya
VEGETARIAN RESTAURANTS

Well over a thousand years ago Buddhists priests in Japan developed an impressive menu of vegetarian dishes, *shōjin ryōri* (show-jeen rio-ree), because they were forbidden to eat meat. *Shōjin ryōri* was served in all Buddhist temples in the country, to priests as well as to visiting laymen. Buddhist temples have traditionally provided overnight lodging for travelers and those wishing a respite from the hectic outside world. A growing health consciousness in Japan in recent decades has resulted in the spread of *shōjin ryōri* beyond the temples to *ryōtei* and health-food restaurants in major cities.

Menu choices in vegetarian restaurants feature the same vegetables served in other Japanese-style restaurants. The primary feature of the *shōjin ryōri-ya* is that they offer full-course meals—including appetizers, soups, main dishes, and desserts—using only vegetables.

39

Shokudō

GENERAL RESTAURANTS

The literal meaning of *shokudō* (show-kuu-doe) is something like food hall or dining room. These relatively inexpensive restaurants are found at airports, in train terminals, department stores, office buildings, and in neighborhood shopping areas. They generally offer a variety of Japanese, Chinese, and Western-style dishes. Larger ones in airports and department stores have extensive menus and some of the best bargain meals in Japan. These restaurants invariably

have display cases or windows exhibiting wax models
of their main dishes and prices.

40

Shokuji-dokoro
"FOOD PLACE" RESTAURANTS

Shokuji-dokoro (show-kuu-jee
doe-koe-roe) means food place and refers to small, unpretentious restaurants serving a half dozen or so of the
more popular Japanese rice and noodle dishes, along
with beer and saké. Also known as *meshi-ya* (may-she-
yah), which means food shop, these restaurants usually
have a counter and stools, plus a few tables or tatami-
mat rooms. In addition to being around transportation
terminals and in neighborhood shopping areas, these
restaurants are found in the basements of office buildings and some older hotels. Following are some of the
dishes that are typically found in *shokuji-dokoro:*

> *buta shōga-yaki* (buu-tah show-gah-yah-kee) Slices of
> pork marinated in soy sauce and ginger, then cooked
> in the same sauce.
>
> *kaki-age* (kah-kee-ah-gay) Small pieces of squid or
> shrimp and vegetables deep-fried and served with a
> soy-sauce dip.
>
> *sashimi teishoku* (sah-she-me tay-show-kuu) A meal of
> raw fish, most often chunks of pink tuna or sea

bream, served on shredded white radish, with rice, a
clear soup, and pickles.

tonkatsu (tone-kot-sue) Breaded, deep-fried pork cutlet.
In some restaurants the pork is cut into small pieces
and is called *hito-kuchi katsu* (ssh-toe-kuu-chee kot-
sue), or bite-size cutlets.

yanagawa-nabe (yah-nah-gah-wah-nah-bay) Loach (small
freshwater fish) mixed with sliced burdock root and
egg, seasoned with sweetened soy sauce, and cooked
in a stoneware bowl.

41

Soba-ya
BUCKWHEAT-NOODLE SHOPS

Soba (so-bah) noodles, made
of buckwheat, originated in mountainous areas of Japan
where people learned how to mix eggs and potato or
some other root starch with buckwheat flour to produce
a dough that would hold together and could be cut into
noodles. These noodles are long and brownish-gray.
Each bowl of *soba* noodles is generally served with a small
side dish of sliced or chopped leeks to be used as a topping. Many diners also sprinkle on a generous portion
of red pepper as a taste enhancer.

Soba-ya, or buckwheat-noodle shops, are usually small
to medium-size shops with a design and decor that are
Japanese style to varying degrees. The more traditional

the decor—which means sliding doors, *noren* curtains outside the doors, classically styled wooden counters and interiors—the higher the class of the shop (and the higher the bill).

Some *soba* shops have been in business for generations, are very exclusive, and cater to an elite clientele that includes top government and business leaders, whose chauffeur-driven limousines regularly block the narrow streets around the shops at noon. Most *soba-ya*, however, are small, unimposing shops on neighborhood shopping streets, around transportation terminals, and in the basements of office and other public buildings.

Soba noodles are served in a broth in a variety of styles, and with ingredients that give the individual versions their names. There are at least thirty different *soba* dishes, served hot or cold, including the following:

cha soba (chah so-bah) Literally tea soba, these are tea-flavored green noodles served cold on a bamboo rack, with a soy-based broth and a tiny dish of sliced leeks and a dab of horseradish. The leeks and horse-radish are mixed in the broth, which serves as a dip for the noodles.

chikara soba (chee-kah-rah so-bah) Pieces of boiled *mochi* in a bowl of noodles.

gomoku soba (go-moe-kuu so-bah) A Chinese dish with pieces of boiled egg, ham, pork, vegetables, and fish cake.

hiyashi kitsune soba (he-yah-she keet-sue-nay so-bah) A summer dish of noodles served cold with pieces of fried tofu.

kake soba (kah-kay so-bah) Noodles in plain broth.

kaki-tama soba (kah-kee-tah-mah so-bah) Noodles in a cornstarch-thickened broth, mixed with an egg.

kamo nanban soba (kah-moe nahn-bahn so-bah) Noodles with pieces of chicken or duck and leeks.

karē nanban soba (kah-ray nahn-bahn so-bah) Noodles in a thick, curry-flavored broth with leeks.

kenchin soba (ken-cheen so-bah) Noodles with pieces of chicken, burdock, taro root, and devil's-tongue gelatin.

kitsune soba (keet-sue-nay so-bah) Noodles with pieces of fried tofu.

mori soba (moe-ree so-bah) Noodles served cold on a bamboo rack, with a soy dip on the side.

niku nanban soba (nee-kuu nahn-bahn so-bah) Noodles with pork and leeks.

okame soba (oh-kah-may so-bah) Noodles with mushrooms, wheat cake, fish cake, and bamboo shoots.

oyako nanban soba (oh-yah-koe nahn-bahn so-bah) Noodles with pieces of chicken, egg, and leeks.

tenpura soba (ten-puu-rah so-bah) Noodles with tempura-fried shrimp.

tenzaru soba (ten-zah-rue so-bah) Noodles served cold with strips of seaweed and pieces of tempura.

tororo soba (toe-roe-roe so-bah) Noodles in a soy-and-fish bouillon, covered with the gooey mountain potato called *tororo,* a raw egg, and dried seaweed.

tsukimi soba (t'sue-kee-me so-bah) Noodles with a raw egg on top.

zaru soba (zah-rue so-bah) Noodles topped with strips of dried seaweed served cold on a bamboo rack, with a soy-based sauce on the side.

zāsai soba (zah-sie so-bah) *Zāsai* is a Chinese pickle
preserved in salt. *Zāsai soba* consists of noodles in a
pork broth flavored with *zāsai,* with bean sprouts,
sliced bamboo shoots, and bits of pork.

One of the most common *soba* dishes is fried noodles,
yaki-soba (yah-kee-so-bah). *Yawarakai yaki-soba* (yah-wah-
rah-kie yah-kee-so-bah) is a helping of noodles lightly
fried with pieces of pork, bean sprouts, carrots, and cabbage. *Katai yaki-soba* (kah-tie yah-kee-so-bah) uses similar ingredients but the noodles are fried until they are
more crisp. *Yaki-soba* is sold at corner stands, in neighborhood restaurants, in department-store cafeterias—
virtually everywhere in Japan.

42

Sui-mono

SOUPS

Japanese soups, called *sui-
mono* (sue-e-moe-no), include clear soups and thicker
soups made with miso. Among the clear soups are:

clam soup *hamaguri sūpu* (hah-mah-guu-ree sue-puu)
diced-shrimp soup *ebi shinjō sūpu* (ay-bee sheen-joe
   sue-puu)
matsutake mushroom soup *matsu-take sūpu* (mot-sue-tah-
   kay sue-puu)

Soups made with miso include:

bean-curd soup *tōfu miso-shiru* (toe-fuu me-so-she-
rue)
freshwater-clam soup *shijimi-jiru* (she-jee-me-jee-rue)
nameko mushroom soup *nameko-shiru* (nah-me-koe-
she-rue)
red-miso soup *akadashi* (ah-kah-dah-she)

Other kinds of soup include:

bean-sprout soup *moyashi sūpu* (moe-yah-she sue-puu)
beef-rib soup *karubi sūpu* (kah-rue-bee sue-puu)
egg soup *tamago sūpu* (tah-mah-go sue-puu)
seaweed soup *wakame sūpu* (wah-kah-may sue-puu)
vegetable soup *yasai sūpu* (yah-sie sue-puu)

43

Sukiyaki-ya
SUKIYAKI RESTAURANTS

After sushi, sukiyaki is per-
haps the most well-known Japanese dish among foreign
visitors, but it has a relatively short history in Japan.
Prior to the fall of the Tokugawa shogunate in 1868,
Buddhism, which was more or less the state religion,
forbade the eating of beef and pork. Even after this religious sanction was lifted, meat was seldom eaten. It was

not until the 1960s and 1970s that beef became a common feature of the Japanese diet.

Originally sukiyaki was another *nabe-mono,* or "pot dish," and only recently achieved the status of a banquet-style meal. In fact, the popularity of the dish among foreign residents and visitors in the 1950s and 1960s played a key role in the popularization of sukiyaki restaurants. Now the dish is served in a variety of Japanese restaurants, including *ryōtei* and steakhouse chains like Suehiro.

Sukiyaki consists of thin slices of beef, along with leeks, tofu, mushrooms, noodles made from devil's-tongue gelatin, and chrysanthemum leaves cooked in a stock flavored with soy sauce, saké, and sugar. Plain white rice and a dip made from beaten raw egg complete the meal. The egg dip cools the hot morsels and gives them a special flavor.

Several varieties of beef are used in sukiyaki, different according to where and how the cattle were raised, fat content of the meat, and type of cut. Generally, only the larger, fancier sukiyaki restaurants offer more than two of the available meat choices. The following are popular:

> beef fillet cut *hire suki-yaki* (he-ray sue-kee-yah-kee)
>
> fat-marbled beef *shimofuri suki-yaki* (she-moe-fuu-ree sue-kee-yah-kee)
>
> Matsuzaka beef (Kobe beef) *Matsuzaka bīfu* (mot-sue-zah-kah bee-fuu)
>
> roast (standard-cut) meat *rōsu suki-yaki* (roe-suu sue-kee-yah-kee)

44

Sunakku
"SNACK BARS"

Sunakku (snock-ku) is a Japanized rendering of the English word snack, but there are big differences between Western snack bars and Japanese *sunakku*. The Japanese version may be just a restaurant or a restaurant that turns into a bar at night.

Sunakku vary in size but are usually rather small. They have menus featuring things like fried chicken, spaghetti, and sandwiches, as well as Japanese dishes. Some *sunakku* are popular places for both lunch and evening meals.

Sunakku that double as bars at night appeared soon after a law was passed in the 1960s establishing an 11 p.m. curfew for bars and nightclubs. Since *sunakku* are registered as restaurants they can stay open twenty-four hours a day.

45

Sushi-ya
SUSHI SHOPS

Αccording to one recent count, in Japan, there are almost fifty thousand *sushi-ya* (sue-she-yah), sushi shops, with some ten thousand in the Tokyo area alone. With their sliding doors, distinctive *noren* curtains, and natural cedar counters, sushi shops are microcosms of traditional Japanese design. But a recent type of *sushi-ya* that incorporates new technology has a counter and seats facing a conveyor belt that carries sushi. At this kind of shop you serve yourself from the line of dishes moving slowly past. You also get your own hot tea from taps above the counter. If you don't find what you want on the conveyor belt, you can call out a special order to one of the chefs. Your bill is determined by how many dishes you have in front of you when you finish, and in the case of some of the more expensive choices, by a color code.

Sushi is usually thought of as raw fish and raw seafood placed on small mounds of rice that have been lightly seasoned with vinegar, sugar, and salt. This is the Tokyo style of sushi, which is known as *nigiri-zushi* (nee-ghee-ree-zuu-she). The Osaka area has its own style of sushi called *oshi-zushi* (oh-she-zuu-she), which consists of marinated or boiled fish placed on top of rice that has been shaped in rectangular wooden molds, then cut into smaller pieces for serving. Sushi shops also serve *sashimi* (sah-she-me), cuts of plain raw fish that are dipped in soy sauce.

There are literally dozens of varieties of sushi, which may vary according to the season, area, etc. Most foreign visitors begin with *maguro* (mah-guu-roe), or tuna, which has a mild taste, then move on to more unusual varieties. Following are popular choices and styles:

aji (ah-jee) horse mackerel

aka-gai (ah-kah-guy) ark shell

anago (ah-nah-go) conger eel, broiled and brushed with a sweet sauce

aoyagi (ah-oh-yah-ghee) round clam

awabi (ah-wah-bee) abalone

buri (buu-ree) yellowtail

chakin-zushi (chah-keen-zuu-she) seasoned rice wrapped in an egg crepe

chirashi-zushi (chee-rah-she-zuu-she) Different kinds of raw or marinated seafood, along with pieces of fish cake, pickled ginger, etc., on a bed of rice in a lacquered box. There are usually two or three of these set sushi meals, varying in quality, size, and price. The smallest, cheapest set is called *nami* (nah-me) or *ume* (uu-may); the middle grade is called *jō* (joe) or *take* (tah-kay); and the most elaborate and expensive is *toku* (toe-kuu) or *matsu* (mot-sue).

chūtoro (chuu-toe-roe) pinkish, slightly fatty tuna

ebi (ay-bee) shrimp

futo-maki (fuu-toe-mah-kee) or *nori maki* (no-ree-mah-kee) seasoned rice and bits of tuna, egg, etc., rolled and wrapped in a sheet of dried seaweed

hamachi (hah-mah-chee) yellowtail

hamaguri (hah-mah-guu-ree) clam

hirame (he-rah-may) flatfish; sole

hotate-gai (hoe-tah-tay-guy) scallop

ika (ee-kah) squid; cuttlefish

ikura (ee-kuu-rah) salmon eggs

inari-zushi (ee-nah-ree-zuu-she) pouch of tofu boiled in a sweet sauce and filled with seasoned rice

iwashi (ee-wah-she) sardine

kajiki (kah-jee-kee) swordfish

kappa-maki (kah-pah-mah-kee) slices of cucumber with a dab of horseradish in seasoned rice, rolled in sheets of dried seaweed

kohada (koe-hah-dah) gizzard shad

maguro no akami (mah-guu-roe no ah-kah-me) red tuna

miru-gai (me-rue-guy) type of round clam that is boiled before being served

odori-ebi (oh-doe-ree-ay-bee) live, "dancing" shrimp

oshinko-maki (oh-sheen-koe-mah-kee) seasoned rice shaped around small slices of pickled radish and wrapped in sheets of dried seaweed

shako (shah-koe) mantis shrimp

suzuki (sue-zuu-kee) sea bass

taira-gai (tie-rah-guy) fan shell

tako (tah-koe) octopus

takuwan-maki (tah-kuu-won-mah-kee) pickled radish in rice wrapped in sheets of dried seaweed

tamago-maki (tah-mah-go-mah-kee) bits of mushroom, other vegetables, and seaweed in seasoned rice, wrapped in an omelette sheet

tarako-maki (tah-rah-koe-mah-kee) codfish eggs in rice wrapped in sheets of dried seaweed

tekka-maki (take-kah-mah-kee) pieces of raw tuna with a dab of horseradish in rice wrapped in sheets of dried seaweed

tori-gai (toe-ree-guy) cockle

uni (uu-nee) eggs of sea urchin

wasabi (wah-sah-bee) a spicy condiment made of freshly
grated or powdered horseradish. The taste may be
too hot for novices. Sushi makers ordinarily put a
dab between the fish and the rice, and some customers stir a bit more into their soy sauce. If you do
not want *wasabi* on your sushi, say *sabi nuki* (sah-bee
nuu-kee), "no horseradish," when you place your
order.

Where you sit in a regular sushi shop determines to
some extent how you order. If you sit at the counter,
you are expected to order your choices individually, call-
ing out the name of the kind you want. One order normally consists of two pieces, which you can eat with your
fingers or with chopsticks.

If you sit at a table you place a single order, naming
the varieties you want, or you order *nigiri-zushi* (nee-
ghee-ree-zuu-she), a set combination of different kinds
of sushi. Most shops have at least two combination sets,
varying in the number and kind of fish. The smaller,
cheaper combination is called *nami* (nah-me). The larger,
more expensive set is called *jō* (joe).

46

Special Sushi Vocabulary

Several foods found in various
restaurants are called by special names in sushi shops.

Agari (ah-gah-ree) literally means complete or come to an end. In sushi shops it means the green tea served at the end of the meal. There is no charge for this tea.

Gari (gah-ree) is the sliced, pickled ginger that is always served with sushi. The regular term for this kind of ginger is *su shōga* (sue show-gah) but in sushi shops it is called *gari,* apparently in reference to the crunching sound it makes when you chew it. *Gari-gari* (gah-ree-gah-ree) means crunchy.

Murasaki (muu-rah-sah-kee), literally purple, is the term for soy sauce in sushi shops. Most diners dip sushi or *sashimi* in soy sauce to enhance its taste.

47

Tenpura-ya
TEMPURA RESTAURANTS

Adapted from a Portuguese dish—the Portuguese were the first Europeans in Japan, in the 1500s—tempura is one of the three Japanese dishes most popular with foreigners, the other two being sukiyaki and sushi. Tempura consists of vegetables, fish, and shellfish coated in a light batter and deep-fried in a light vegetable oil. The various pieces are usually dipped in a mild soy-based sauce but this is optional.

The true taste of tempura comes through only when it is eaten without sauce or condiments.

Virtually any kind of vegetable or seafood can be fixed tempura style, but the selection at any given time often depends on the season. Following are popular fish and seafood choices:

conger eel *anago* (ah-nah-go)
freshwater smelt *wakasagi* (wah-kah-sah-ghee)
prawn *kuruma-ebi* (kuu-rue-mah-ay-bee)
scallop *hotate-gai* (hoe-tah-tay-guy)
shrimp *ebi* (ay-bee)
sillago fish *kisu* (kee-sue)
squid *ika* (ee-kah)

The following vegetables are often used in tempura:

asparagus *asupara* (ah-sue-pah-rah)
burdock root *gobō* (go-boe)
carrot *ninjin* (neen-jeen)
chrysanthemum leaf *shungiku no ha* (shune-ghee-kuu no hah)
dried seaweed *nori* (no-ree)
eggplant *nasu* (nah-sue)
green pepper *pīman* (pee-mahn)
onion *tamanegi* (tah-mah-nay-ghee)
shiitake mushroom *shī-take* (she-e-tah-kay)
squash *kabocha* (kah-boe-chah)
sweet potato *satsuma imo* (sot-sue-mah ee-moe)

48

Teppanyaki-ya
GRILLED-STEAK RESTAURANTS

Teppan-yaki (tep-pahn-yah-kee) is the style of table-grill cooking made famous in the U.S. by the Benihana chain. Pieces of meat, seafood, and vegetables are quickly grilled by a chef at the diner's table. The dicing of the ingredients, the special soy and garlic sauces, and the quick frying give this style of cooking its special appeal. In addition to high-grade beef, common *teppan-yaki* ingredients are mushrooms, onions, green peppers, bean sprouts, scallops, squid, and prawns. A popular variation of the standard *teppan-yaki* is *batā-yaki* (bah-tah-yah-kee), or cooking in butter.

The term *teppan-yaki* is also used to mean American-style steakhouses, where the steaks are grilled whole, either in the restaurant kitchen or on large charcoal grills in the dining room. Several cuts of meat are normally available in *teppan-yaki* restaurants, including tenderloin, sirloin, filet mignon, and sometimes veal. The typical restaurant menu consists of set lunches or dinners featuring one of the above meat cuts, soup, rice, and usually a fruit dessert. A "mixed grill" includes a portion of steak along with either shrimp, scallops, or squid, and a variety of vegetables. Following is a list of the common choices in this style of dining:

fillet steak *hire sutēki* (he-ray stay-kee)

sirloin steak *sāroin sutēki* (sah-royne stay-kee)

tenderloin steak *tendāroin sutēki* (ten-dah-royne stay-kee)

veal steak *ko-ushi sutēki* (koe-uu-shee stay-kee)

mixed grill *mikkusu guriru* (meek-kuu-sue guu-ree-rue)

salad *sarada* (sah-rah-dah)

seasonal vegetable combination *kisetsu no yasai moriawase*
(kee-sate-sue no yah-sie moe-ree-ah-wah-say)

49

Tonkatsu-ya

PORK-CUTLET RESTAURANTS

Another instant hit with most visitors to Japan is *ton-katsu* (tone-kot-sue), literally pork cutlet, but the Japanese version takes pork to a new high. Choice cuts of pork are breaded in a rich batter, deep-fried, and served with shredded cabbage, soup, rice, and pickles. Specialty *ton-katsu* restaurants, like Tonki in Tokyo's Meguro district, have national followings because of the distinctive taste of their batter and the quality of the meat they use. *Ton-katsu* dishes, almost invariably of lesser quality, are also served in other restaurants, including *shokudō, shokuji-dokoro,* and Western-style places.

Tonkatsu-ya generally have several versions of pork cutlet on their menus. The following are common:

hire-katsu (he-ray-kot-sue) very lean fillet cut of pork, the best in the shop

rōsu-katsu (roe-suu-kot-sue) lean cut of pork, but with some fat left on

hito-kuchi hire-katsu (ssh-toe-kuu-chee he-ray-kot-sue) lean pork fillet cut and cooked in bite sizes

kushi-katsu (kuu-she-kot-sue) chunks of pork and leeks deep-fried on skewers

katsu-jū (kot-sue-juu) pieces of pork cutlet served on a dish or bowl of rice

Other dishes on the menus of *ton-katsu* restaurants include:

chicken cutlet *chikin-katsu* (chee-keen-kot-sue)

crab croquette *kani korokke* (kah-nee koe-roke-kay)

ground-meat patty *menchi-katsu* (men-chee-kot-sue)

horse mackerel *aji furai* (ah-jee fuu-rye)

oysters *kaki furai* (kah-kee fuu-rye)

potato croquette *poteto korokke* (poe-tay-toe koe-roke-kay)

shrimp *ebi furai* (ay-bee fuu-rye)

50

Unagi-ya

EEL RESTAURANTS

Unagi (uu-nah-ghee), eel, charcoal-broiled and seasoned with a delicately sweetened sauce, is one of the gourmet dishes of Japan. Considered a delicacy, it tends to be on the expensive side. Eel is popular all year but is traditionally eaten during the hottest summer days because it is believed to provide extra stamina during the heat. There is also a widespread belief that eel is an aphrodisiac.

Better *unagi-ya* keep their eels alive until just before they are cooked. The eel is then cut open and the bones removed. In the Tokyo area it is grilled, steamed, and grilled again. In the Osaka-Kobe district the steaming is omitted to make the meat crispier. During the cooking process, the eel fillets are repeatedly brushed with a sweet, piquant sauce.

Unagi is served a la carte or as a set meal including soup, rice, and pickles. An a la carte serving, called *unagi donburi* (uu-nah-ghee done-buu-ree), consists of a filleted section of eel on top of a bowl of rice. Other eel dishes include the following:

ikada-yaki (ee-kah-dah-yah-kee) grilled eel fillets lined up side-by-side and skewered

kaba-yaki (kah-bah-yah-kee) grilled eel on skewers without rice

kimo sui (kee-moe sue-e) eel-liver soup

kimo-yaki (kee-moe-yah-kee) grilled eel livers, with grated radish

shira-yaki (she-rah-yah-kee) "white" eel, grilled without sauce

u-maki (uu-mah-kee) grilled eel wrapped in a sheet of cooked egg

unagi-zushi (uu-nah-ghee-zuu-she) broiled eel fixed sushi
   style

una-jū (uu-nah-juu) large serving of grilled eel on rice,
   usually in a lacquered box

unatama-jū (uu-nah-tah-mah-juu) eel and egg served on
   rice

51

Yakitori-ya

SKEWERED-CHICKEN RESTAURANTS

Even more conspicuous than
Japan's thousands of sushi shops are the *yakitori-ya* (yah-
kee-toe-ree-yah), skewered-chicken shops, with their
large, red lanterns, *noren* curtains, and barbecue aroma.
These restaurants range in size and style from crude outdoor stands beneath elevated train tracks to gourmet
shops in prestigious geisha districts like Akasaka in Tokyo
and Pontocho in Kyoto.

A visit to a *yakitori-ya* is more than a trip to a restaurant to get something to eat. Drinking beer or saké goes
with eating *yaki-tori,* and a party mood and atmosphere
are part of the overall ambience of the *yakitori-ya.* People go to socialize as much as to eat.

Yaki-tori itself consists of chunks of skewered chick-
en, leeks, and other vegetables salted and grilled, or
grilled in a special barbecue sauce over a charcoal fire.

This distinctive sauce is called *tare* (tah-ray). Another popular condiment, made of red pepper and other spices, called *shichimi* (she-chee-me), is available for those who like to spice up their meal. Among the more popular *yaki-tori* choices are the following:

chicken, boneless with skin *shō-niku* (show-nee-kuu)
chicken breast without skin *sasami* (sah-sah-me)
chicken chunks with leeks *hasami* (hah-sah-me)
chicken giblets *motsu* (moat-sue)
chicken gizzards *suna-gimo* (sue-nah-ghee-moe)
chicken hearts *hatsu* (hot-sue)
chicken leg *momo-yaki* (moe-moe-yah-kee)
chicken liver *rebā* (ray-bah)
chicken liver with other giblets *tori kimo-yaki* (toe-ree kee-moe-yah-kee)
chicken meatballs *tsukune* (t'sue-kuu-nay)
chicken pieces with ligaments *nankotsu* (nahn-kot-sue)
chicken wing *te-basaki* (tay-bah-sah-kee)
chicken with bones *hone-tsuki* (hoe-nay-t'sue-kee)

Vegetables commonly found in *yakitori-ya* include:

gingko nuts *ginnan* (gheen-nahn)
green pepper *pīman* (pee-mahn)
leek *naganegi* (nah-gah-nay-ghee)
onion *tamanegi* (tah-mah-nay-ghee)
shiitake mushroom *shī-take* (she-e-tah-kay)
vegetable sampler *yasai-yaki* (yah-sie-yah-kee)

52

Desserts

Although formal meals may be topped off with fresh fruit, Japanese do not normally end meals with pastry desserts like pie or cake. Most traditional desserts as well as Western-style desserts in Japan are eaten as snacks between meals in coffee shops or traditional sweets shops known as *kanmi-ya*. Following are some of the more popular desserts:

abekawa mochi (ah-bay-kah-wah moe-chee) *Mochi* is a thick dough made from pounded, glutinous rice. The dough is cut into small cakes, then boiled, broiled, or grilled. In *abekawa mochi,* the cakes are sprinkled with sweetened bean powder that is yellowish in color.

iso-maki (ee-so-mah-kee) Grilled *mochi* seasoned with soy sauce and wrapped in dried sheets of seaweed. This dish is considered a dessert although it is not sweet.

shiruko (she-ruu-koe) pieces of *mochi* in a small lacquered bowl of sweetened bean-paste soup

zenzai (zen-zie) bean jam with boiled *mochi*

anmitsu (ahn-meet-sue) This traditional dessert consists of cubes of a gelatin-like substance made from agar-agar, sweetened bean paste, and a few pieces of fruit, often canned. The mixture is topped with syrup or a honey mixture.

kurīmu anmitsu (kuu-ree-muu ahn-meet-sue) *anmitsu* with a scoop of vanilla ice cream

furūtsu mitsumame (fuu-root-sue meet-sue-mah-may) Similar to *anmitsu,* this dish is made of cubes of agar-agar gelatin, sweetened whole beans, pieces of fruit, and rice candy, with a syrupy topping.

kurīmu mitsumame (kuu-ree-muu meet-sue-mah-may) *furūtsu mitsumame* with a scoop of vanilla ice cream

furūtsu kurēpu (fuu-root-sue kuu-ray-puu) a crepe with fruit filling

kōri azuki (koe-ree ah-zuu-kee) Shaved ice over a small scoop of sweetened bean jam, covered with syrup. A dab of bean jam is sometimes used as a topping.

kōri ichigo (koe-ree ee-chee-go) shaved ice with strawberry syrup

kōri meron (koe-ree may-roan) shaved ice with melon-flavored syrup

kōri miruku (koe-ree me-ruu-kuu) shaved ice with sweetened milk

kōri remon (koe-ree ray-moan) shaved ice with lemon-flavored syrup

uji kintoki (uu-jee keen-toe-kee) shaved ice over sweetened bean paste, covered with green-tea syrup

orenji yōguruto (oh-rane-jee yoe-guu-rue-toe) orange-flavored yogurt

pain yōguruto (pine yoe-guu-rue-toe) pineapple-flavored yogurt

ichigo yōguruto (ee-chee-go yoe-guu-rue-toe) strawberry-flavored yogurt

purin (puu-reen) A vanilla-flavored egg custard sweetened with brown sugar, topped with whipped cream. Slices of tangerine are often added to the dish.

Desserts more familiar to Westerners are also now widely available in Japan. Thousands of bakeries, many of which are self-service, produce a wide variety of Western-style pastries. Ice-cream shops, including several well-known American chains, are also plentiful.

53

Street Vendors

Japan has a long tradition of street vendors selling their wares from carts and stands. The tradition became a national phenomenon shortly after the establishment of the Tokugawa shogunate in Edo (Tokyo) in 1603. In the 1630s, the third Tokugawa shogun instituted a system that required some 250 of feudal Japan's provincial lords, known as *daimyō* (di-me-yoe), to come to Edo every other year to serve at his court.

Each *daimyō* was required to bring with him a large retinue of personal servants, retainers, and samurai warriors. The larger the lord's fief, the larger the retinue he was required to bring. Since all regular travel in Japan was by foot, thousands of people were marching up and down Japan's main roads at any time. All these people were customers for roadside stands. Another key factor in the development of so many food vendors was the presence of thousands of temples and shrines around the country. Each year these temples and shrines sponsored festivals, events that attracted large numbers of people, who in turn attracted vendors of all kinds. Today some of the more popular street-vendor foods include the following:

ama-guri (ah-mah-guu-ree) sweet chestnuts roasted over hot pebbles

mitarashi dango (me-tah-rah-she dahn-go) rice-flour dumplings charcoal-broiled and coated with soy sauce

oden (oh-den) Japanese-style stew

okonomi-yaki (oh-koe-no-me-yah-kee) "Japanese quiche"

yaki-imo (yah-kee-ee-moe) baked yam

yaki-soba (yah-kee-so-bah) fried noodles

yaki-tori (yah-kee-to-ree) skewered pieces of charbroiled chicken

Particularly at temple festivals, which attract children as well as adults, dessert-type sweets like the following are popular:

bekkō ame (bake-koe ah-may) a sugared sucker

mikan bekkō (me-kahn bake-koe) candied tangerine served on a stick

okoshi (oh-koe-she) popped rice in various doll-like shapes coated with sugar

wata-gashi (wah-tah-gah-she) cotton candy

54

Diner's Vocabulary

The following list of English words and their Japanese counterparts should enable you to eat and drink with ease during your stay in Japan:

abalone *awabi* (ah-wah-bee)
adzuki bean *azuki* (ah-zuu-kee)
agar-agar *kanten* (kahn-ten)
a la carte *ippin ryōri* (eep-peen rio-ree)
anchovy *anchobī* (ahn-choe-bee)
angler fish *ankō* (ahn-koe)
appetizer *tsumami* (t'sue-mah-me); *ōdoburu* (oh-doe-buu-rue)
apple *ringo* (reen-go)
apple pie *appuru pai* (ahp-puu-rue pie)
apricot *anzu* (ahn-zuu)
ark shell *aka-gai* (ah-kah-guy)
asparagus *asuparagasu* (ahss-pah-rah-gah-sue)
Atka mackerel *hokke* (hoke-kay)
au gratin *guratan* (guu-rah-tahn)
bacon *bēkon* (bay-kone)
bad tasting *mazui* (mah-zuu-ee)
bamboo shoot *takenoko* (tah-kay-no-koe)
banana *banana* (bah-nah-nah)
barracuda *kamasu* (kah-mah-sue)

bean *mame* (mah-may)

bean curd (soybean) *tōfu* (toe-fuu)

bean sprout *moyashi* (moe-yah-she)

beef *bīfu* (bee-fuu); *gyūniku* (g'yune-nee-kuu)

beer *bīru* (bee-rue)

beverage *nomi-mono* (no-me-moe-no)

bitter *nigai* (nee-guy)

bitter orange *daidai* (die-die)

black-eyed pea *sasage* (sah-sah-gay)

black pepper *koshō* (koe-show)

black tea *kōcha* (koe-chah)

blowfish (globefish) *fugu* (fuu-guu)

blueberry *burūberī* (buu-rue-bay-ree)

bluefish *mutsu* (moot-sue)

bonito *katsuo* (kot-sue-oh)

box lunch *bentō* (ben-toe)

brandy *burandē* (buu-rahn-day)

bread *pan* (pahn)

breakfast *asa gohan* (ah-sah go-hahn)

broccoli *burokkorī* (buu-roke-koe-ree)

Brussels sprouts *me-kyabetsu* (may-k'yah-bet-sue)

buckwheat noodles *soba* (so-bah)

burdock *gobō* (go-boe)

butter *batā* (bah-tah)

butterfish *mana-gatsuo* (mah-nah-got-sue-oh)

cabbage *kyabetsu* (k'yah-bet-sue)

cake *kēki* (kay-kee)

canned food *kanzume* (kahn-zuu-may)

canned tuna *tsuna* (t'sue-nah)

carp *koi* (koy)

carrot *ninjin* (neen-jeen)

cauliflower *karifurawā* (kah-ree-fuu-rah-wahh)

celery *serorī* (say-roe-ree)

chair *isu* (e-sue)

charcoal-broiled chicken on skewers *yaki-tori* (yah-kee-toe-ree)

cheese *chīzu* (chee-zuu)

cherry *sakuranbō* (sah-kuu-rahn-boe)

chestnut *kuri* (kuu-ree)

chicken *chikin* (chee-keen); *tori* (toe-ree)

chicken meatball *tsukune* (t'sue-kuu-nay)

Chinese cabbage *hakusai* (hah-kuu-sie)

Chinese dumpling, fried *gyōza* (g'yoe-zah)

Chinese dumpling, steamed *shūmai* (shuu-my)

Chinese noodles *rāmen* (rah-men)

Chinese pickle *zāsai* (zah-sie)

Chinese-soup spoon *renge* (ren-gay)

Chinese-style *Chūkafū* (chuu-kah-fuu)

chives *asatsuki* (ah-sot-sue-kee)

chocolate *chokorēto* (choe-koe-ray-toe)

chopsticks *hashi* (hah-she)

chopsticks, disposable *waribashi* (wah-ree-bah-she)

clam *hamaguri* (hah-mah-guu-ree)

clear soup *sumashi* (sue-mah-she)

club soda *tansan* (tahn-sahn)

cockle *tori-gai* (toe-ree-guy)

cocktail *kakuteru* (kah-kuu-tay-rue)

cocktail snack *tsuki-dashi* (ski-dah-she)

cocoa *kokoa* (koe-koe-ah)

coconut *kokonatsu* (koe-koe-not-sue)

cod *tara* (tah-rah)

cod roe *tarako* (tah-rah-koe)

coffee *kōhī* (koe-he)

coffee shop *kissaten* (kees-sah-ten)

cognac *konyakku* (kone-yahk-kuu)

cola *kōra* (koe-rah)

cold (served cold) *hiyashi* (he-yah-she)

conger eel *anago* (ah-nah-go)

cook (chef) *kokku* (koke-kuu)

cooked rice *gohan* (go-hahn)

cookie *kukkī* (kook-kee)

corn *kōn* (kone)

crab *kani* (kah-nee)

cream *kurīmu* (kuu-ree-muu)

crepe *kurēpu* (kuu-ray-puu)

croquette *korokke* (koe-roke-kay)

Crucian carp *funa* (fuu-nah)

cucumber *kyūri* (que-ree)

cuisine (cooking, food) *ryōri* (rio-ree)

cup *koppu* (kope-puu)

curry *karē* (kah-ray)

deep-fried *age* (ah-gay)

deep-fried cutlet *katsu* (kot-sue)

deep-fried tidbits on skewers *kushi-age* (kuu-she-ah-gay)

deer *shika* (she-kah)

delicious *oishii* (oh-e-shee)

delivery service *demae* (day-my)

dessert *dezāto* (day-zot-toe)

devil's-tongue gelatin *konnyaku* (kone-yah-kuu)

devil's-tongue noodles *shira-taki* (she-rah-tah-kee)

dinner *yūshoku* (yuu-show-kuu)

draft beer *nama bīru* (nah-mah bee-rue)

dried bonito *katsuo-bushi* (kot-sue-oh-buu-she)

dried fish *hi-mono* (he-moe-no)

dried roe *karasumi* (kah-rah-sue-me)

dried seaweed (laver) *nori* (no-ree)

drink *nomi-mono* (no-me-moe-no)

drinking place *nomi-ya* (no-me-yah)

duck *kamo* (kah-moe)

dumpling *dango* (dahn-go)

eel *unagi* (uu-nah-ghee)

egg *tamago* (tah-mah-go)

egg custard stew *chawan-mushi* (chah-won-muu-she)

eggplant *nasu* (nah-sue)

egg roll *haru-maki* (hah-rue-mah-kee)

egg yolk *kimi* (kee-me)

fillet *hire* (he-ray)

fish *sakana* (sah-kah-nah)

fish cake, deep-fried *satsuma-age* (sot-sue-mah-ah-gay)

fish cake, made from shark *suji* (sue-jee)

fish cake, made from yam *hanpen* (hahn-pen)

fish cake, served in stew and soup *kamaboko* (kah-mah-boe-koe)

fish cake, tube-shaped *chikuwa* (chee-kuu-wah)

flavor *aji* (ah-jee)

flounder (flatfish) *hirame* (he-rah-may)

flying fish *tobiuo* (toe-bee-uu-oh)

food *tabe-mono* (tah-bay-moe-no)

fork *fōku* (foe-kuu)

freshwater shrimp *kawa-ebi* (kah-wah-ay-bee)

freshwater smelt *wakasagi* (wah-kah-sah-ghee)

fruit *kuda-mono* (kuu-dah-moe-no)

full-course meal *kōsu* (koe-sue)

garlic *ninniku* (neen-nee-kuu)

gin *jin* (jeen)

ginger *shōga* (show-gah)

gingko nut *ginnan* (gheen-nahn)

gizzard *sunagimo* (sue-nah-ghee-moe)

gizzard shad fish *kohada* (koe-hah-dah)

glass *gurasu* (guu-rah-sue)

goby fish *haze* (hah-zay)

grape *budō* (buu-doe)

grapefruit *gurēpu-furūtsu* (guu-rape-fuu-root-sue)

grated yam *tororo* (toe-roe-roe)

grated yam over raw tuna *yamakake* (yah-mah-kah-kay)

green leaf used in sukiyaki *shungiku* (shune-ghee-kuu)

green pepper *pīman* (pee-mahn)

green tea *o-cha* (oh-cha); *nihon-cha* (nee-hoan-chah)

grilled giblets *motsu-yaki* (mote-sue-yah-kee)

ground meat *hiki-niku* (he-kee-nee-kuu)

halfbeak fish *sayori* (sah-yoe-ree)

ham *hamu* (hah-muu)

hamburger *hanbāgā* (hahn-bah-gah)

hangover *futsuka-yoi* (futes-kah-yoe-e)

herring *nishin* (nee-sheen)

herring roe *kazu-no-ko* (kah-zuu-no-koe)

honey *hachi-mitsu* (hah-chee-meet-sue)

hungry (I'm hungry) *onaka ga suite imasu* (oh-nah-kah gah t'sue-tay e-mahss)

ice cream *aisu-kurīmu* (aye-sue-kuu-ree-muu)

iced coffee *aisu-kōhī* (aye-sue-koe-he)

Japanese horseradish *wasabi* (wah-sah-bee)

Japanese mustard *karashi* (kah-rah-she)

Japanese pickle *tsukemono* (skay-moe-no)

Japanese radish *daikon* (die-kone)

knife *naifu* (nie-fuu)

lamb *ramu* (rah-muu)

lemon *remon* (ray-moan)

lentil *renzu-mame* (ren-zuu-mah-may)

lettuce *retasu* (ray-tah-sue)

lime *raimu* (rye-muu)

loach *dojō* (doe-joe)

lobster *ise-ebi* (ee-say-ay-bee)

long green onion *naganegi* (nah-gah-nay-ghee)

loquat *biwa* (bee-wah)

lotus root *hasu* (hah-sue); *renkon* (ren-kone)

lychee *raichi* (rye-chee); *reishi* (ray-she)

mackerel *saba* (sah-bah)

mackerel, marinated in vinegar *shime-saba* (she-may-sah-bah)

mandarin orange *mikan* (me-kahn)

mango *mangō* (mahn-go)

mantis shrimp *shako* (shah-koe)

mayonnaise *mayonēzu* (mah-yoe-nay-zuu)

meal *shokuji* (show-kuu-jee)

meat *niku* (nee-kuu)

melon *meron* (may-rone)

menu *menyū* (men-yuu)

milk *gyūnyū* (g'yune-yuu); *miruku* (me-rue-kuu)

muscat grape *masukatto* (mahss-kot-toe)

mushroom *masshurūmu* (mah-shuu-ruu-muu)

nut *nattsu* (not-sue)

octopus *tako* (tah-koe)

olive *orību* (oh-ree-buu)

onion *tamanegi* (tah-mah-nay-ghee)

orange *orenji* (oh-ren-jee)

outdoor food stall *yatai* (yah-tie)

pancake *pankēki* (pahn-kay-kee)

papaya *papaiya* (pah-pie-yah)

parsley *paseri* (pah-say-ree)

pea *endō-mame* (en-doe-mah-may); *gurīn pīsu* (guu-reen pee-su)

peach *momo* (moe-moe)

persimmon *kaki* (kah-kee)

pickled ~ ~-*zuke* (zuu-kay)

pickled Japanese radish *takuan* (tah-kuu-ahn)

pineapple *painappuru* (pine-ahp-puu-rue)

plate *sara* (sah-rah)

plum *puramu* (puu-rah-muu)

pompano (horse mackerel) *aji* (ah-jee)

pork *buta-niku* (buu-tah-nee-kuu)

potato *jagaimo* (jah-guy-moe); *poteto* (poe-tay-toe)

powdered green tea *matcha* (mot-chah)

prune *purun* (puu-rune)

pub *pabu* (pah-buu)

pumpkin *kabocha* (kah-boe-chah)

quail *uzura* (uu-zuu-rah)

quail egg *uzura tamago* (uu-zuu-rah tah-mah-go)

rainbow trout *niji-masu* (nee-jee-mah-sue)

raisin *hoshi-budō* (hoe-she-buu-doe)

recommendation *susume* (sue-sue-may)

red-bean jelly *yōkan* (yoe-kahn)

red pickle, served with rice dishes *fukujin-zuke* (fuu-kuu-jeen-zuu-kay)

red snapper (sea bream) *tai* (tie)

red tilefish *ama-dai* (ah-mah-die)

reserved *yoyaku-zumi* (yoe-yah-kuu-zuu-me)

restaurant, Western-style *restoran* (res-toe-rahn)

restroom *o-tearai* (oh-tay-ah-rye)

rice, boiled *gohan* (go-hahn)

rice, uncooked *kome* (koe-may)

rice ball, wrapped in seaweed *o-nigiri* (oh-nee-ghee-ree)

rice cake *mochi* (moe-chee)

rice cracker *senbei* (sen-bay)

rice cracker, pellet-shaped *arare* (ah-rah-ray)

rice cracker, spicy *kara-senbei* (kah-rah-sen-bay)

rice gruel *o-kayu* (oh-kah-yuu)

rice wine *sake* (sah-kay); *nihon-shu* (nee-hoan-shuu)

roasted chestnut *ama-guri* (ah-mah-guu-ree)

round clam *aoyagi* (ah-oh-yah-ghee)

rum *ramu* (rah-muu)

salmon *sake* (sah-kay); *shake* (shah-kay)

salmon roe *ikura* (e-kuu-rah)

salt *shio* (she-oh)

salty *shio-karai* (she-oh-kah-rye)

sandwich *sandoitchi* (sahn-doe-ee-chee)

sardine *iwashi* (ee-wah-she)

sauce for basting *tare* (tah-ray)

saucer *ko-sara* (koe-sah-rah)

saury fish *sanma* (sahn-mah)

sausage *sōsēji* (soe-say-jee)

scallion (leek) *nira* (nee-rah)

scallop *hotate-gai* (hoe-tah-tay-guy)

sea bass *suzuki* (sue-zuu-kee)

sea urchin roe *uni* (uu-nee)

seaweed, generic *kaisō* (kie-so)

seaweed, long *wakame* (wah-kah-may)

sesame seed *goma* (go-mah)

set meal *teishoku* (tay-show-kuu)

share a table *aiseki* (aye-say-kee)

shark *fuka* (fuu-kah); *same* (sah-may)

shellfish *kai* (kie)

shiitake mushroom *shī-take* (she-e-tah-kay)

shochu liquor *shōchū* (show-chuu)

short-necked clam *asari* (ah-sah-ree)

shrimp *ebi* (ay-bee)

shrimp, small *ko-ebi* (koe-ay-bee)

side dish *o-kazu* (oh-kah-zuu)

sillago fish *kisu* (kee-sue)

snack, eaten while drinking *o-tsumami* (oh-t'sue-mah-me)

sole *shita-birame* (ssh-tah-bee-rah-may)

soup *sūpu* (sue-puu)

soup made with soybean paste *miso-shiru* (me-so-she-rue)

sour *suppai* (supe-pie)

soybean *daizu* (die-zuu)

soybean, fermented *nattō* (not-toe)

soybean, green *eda-mame* (eh-dah-mah-may)

soybean curd *tōfu* (toe-fuu)

soybean paste *miso* (me-so)

soy sauce *shōyu* (show-yuu)

spaghetti *supagetti* (spah-geh-tee)

Spanish mackerel *sawara* (sah-wah-rah)

sparrow *suzume* (sue-zuu-may)

special (high) grade *jō* (joe)

spice *kōshin-ryō* (koe-sheen-rio)

spicy cod roe *mentaiko* (men-tie-koe)

spinach *hōren-sō* (hoe-ren-so)

spoon *supūn* (sue-poon)

squid *ika* (e-kah)

steak *sutēki* (stay-kee)

stew, Japanese-style *ni-komi* (nee-koe-me)

stew, Western-style *shichū* (she-chuu)

stew made with angler fish *ankō-nabe* (ahn-koe-nah-bay)

stew made with oysters and soybean paste *dote-nabe* (doe-tay-nah-bay)

stir-fried *itame* (ee-tah-may)

strawberry *ichigo* (ee-chee-go)

string bean *ingen-mame* (een-gen-mah-may)

strong flavored *koi* (koy)

sugar *satō* (sah-toe)

surf clam *miru-gai* (me-rue-guy)

sweet *amai* (ah-my)

sweetfish *ayu* (ah-yuu)

sweet potato *satsuma-imo* (sot-sue-mah-ee-moe)

swordfish *kajiki* (kah-jee-kee)

takeout *mochi-kaeri* (moe-chee-kie-ree); *tēku-auto* (take-ow-toe)

tangerine *mikan* (me-kahn)

tofu, cubed in spicy meat sauce *mābō-dōfu* (mah-boe-doe-fuu)

tofu, deep-fried and served in broth *age-dōfu* (ah-gay-doe-fuu)

tofu, grilled *atsu-age* (aht-sue-ah-gay)

tofu, simmered in hot water *yu-dōfu* (yuu-doe-fuu)

toothpick *ha no yōji* (hah no yoe-jee)

trout *masu* (mah-sue)

tuna *maguro* (mah-guu-roe)

turbot *karei* (kah-ray-e)

vanilla *banira* (bah-nee-rah)

vegetable *yasai* (yah-sie)

vodka *uokka* (wahk-kah)

waiter *uētā* (way-tah)

waitress *uētoresu* (way-toe-rase)

water *mizu* (me-zuu)

water, cold *o-hiya* (oh-hee-yah)

water, hot *o-yu* (oh-yuu)
water chestnut *kuwai* (kuu-wie)
watermelon *suika* (sue-e-kah)
weak flavored *usui* (uu-sue-e)
Western food *yōshoku* (yoe-show-kuu)
Western-style *yōfū* (yoe-fuu)
whale *kujira* (kuu-jee-rah)
white radish *daikon* (die-kone)
wine *budō-shu* (buu-doe-shuu); *wain* (wine)
wood-ear (tree fungus) *kikurage* (kee-kuu-rah-gay)
yellowtail fish *buri* (buu-ree)
yogurt *yōguruto* (yoe-guu-ruu-toe)

55

Common Ingredients

A number of ingredients appear in many different Japanese dishes. Although these ingredients are defined in the text, the definitions are repeated here for handy reference.

kamaboko (kah-mah-boe-koe) fish cake
konnyaku (kone-yah-kuu) devil's-tongue gelatin
matsu-take (mat-sue-tah-kay) large mushroom, sometimes called pine mushroom
mirin (mee-reen) sweet saké used for cooking

miso (me-so) fermented soybean paste used for soups, sauces, etc.

mochi (mo-chee) glutinous rice cake

nattō (naht-toe) fermented soybeans

nori (noe-ree) sheet of dried seaweed used to wrap rolls of sushi

shī-take (she-tah-kay) kind of mushroom

shōyu (show-yuu) soy sauce

tōfu (toe-fuu) bean curd

wasabi (wah-sah-bee) Japanese horseradish

Also from YENBOOKS

QUICK-GUIDES

Businessman's

GUIDE
TO
JAPAN

Opening Doors . . .
and Closing Deals!

Boye De Mente

ISBN 0-8048-1613-1 $5.95   ¥590

YENBOOKS

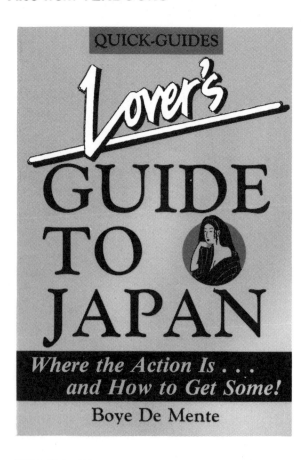